PR
2819
.M37
1987

Martin, William F.,
1933-

The indissoluble
knot

$16.75

DATE			

THE INDISSOLUBLE KNOT

King Lear As
Ironic Drama

William F. Martin

UNIVERSITY
PRESS OF
AMERICA

Lanham • New York • London

Copyright © 1987 by

University Press of America,® Inc.

4720 Boston Way
Lanham, MD 20706

3 Henrietta Street
London WC2E 8LU England

Printed in the United States of America

British Cataloging in Publication Information Available

ISBN: 0-8191-6604-9 (alk. paper)

All University Press of America books are produced on acid-free
paper which exceeds the minimum standards set by the National
Historical Publication and Records Commission.

Dedicated to

My Brothers

and

Ruth

THE INDISSOLUBLE KNOT

TABLE OF CONTENTS

CHAPTER I

INTRODUCTION

King Lear, perhaps more than any other Shakespearean tragedy, has aroused paradoxical commentary. Acclaimed by many scholars and critics as Shakespeare's most remarkable tragedy, it has also been derided as structurally weak, as unrealistic and artificial in its dramatic development, and as abounding in anachronisms, incongruities, inconsistencies, and superfluous characters. No play has evoked more argument about the intentions or the abilities of William Shakespeare. No other Shakespearean drama has given rise to so much critical controversy regarding its merits. Highly respectable critics seemingly cannot agree about the play; contradictory evaluations are so rife that one, if he seriously regards the opinions of the critics, is dismayed to discover a confused medley of antithetical assertions defying one's most adroit intellectual endeavors to effect any satisfactory appraisal of the play.

Notable critical controversy has arisen concerning Shakespeare's alleged failure to achieve thematic unity in Lear. Some authorities contend that through its double plot and by the dramatic looseness of its incidental elements, the play is one in which Shakespeare has attenuated the tragic concentration resident in more typical tragedies. John Middleton Murry, for example, deplores Shakespeare's use of the thematic material in *King Lear:*

> . . . In the handling of the theme . . . Shakespeare was, if not perfunctory, at least uncertain. I could almost believe that Shakespeare was on the verge of madness himself when he wrote *King Lear* . . . . in *King Lear,* I find disturbance, hesitation, uncertainty, and a constant interruption of the "predominant passion." The imagination of the theme becomes perfunctory or strained, the imagination of the verse spasmodic. There is weariness, and a flagging of the invention. *King Lear* makes upon me the impression of the work of a Shakespeare who is out of his depth.[1]

---

[1] John Middleton Murry, Shakespeare (London: Jonathan Cape, 1936), p. 338.

Murry adds that *King Lear* is a work of a man "struggling with an obsession." He believes that the great English tragic poet was unable to cope with the complexities of the *Lear* universe, that he had become the victim of its complexities rather than their master.

Observe now a contradictory evaluation from the renowned poet and Shakespearean critic, Algernon Swinburne:

> The dramatic skill of the supreme dramatic rather than theatrical artist was never more triumphantly manifest than in the fusion and transfiguration of the two [plots] here so naturally and cunningly interwoven. To have turned the ugly and unmanageable legend of Cordelia's suicide in person into the glory of a martyrdom unmatched for its tragic effect of terror and of pity, to have made its inevitable consequence the agony which now strikes out not the reason but the life of her father, is the supreme feat of Shakespeare as a spiritual craftsman.[2]

To note the disagreement of Leo Tolstoy and George Orwell is to realize even more fully the radical divergence of opinions concerning the play. Tolstoy states:

> Such is this celebrated drama. However absurd it appears in my rendering (which I have endeavored to make as impartial as possible), I may confidently say that in the original it is yet more absurd. For any man of our time—if he were not under the hypnotic suggestion that this drama is the height of perfection—it would be enough to read it to its end (were he to have sufficient patience for this) in order to be convinced that, far from being the height of perfection, it is a very bad, carelessly composed production, which, if it could have been of interest to a certain public at a certain time, cannot evoke amongst us anything but aversion and weariness.
> . . . In this, as in the other dramas of Shakespeare, all the characters live, think, speak, and act quite unconformably with the given time and place. . . .It is possible that such

---

[2]Algernon Charles Swinburne, *Shakespeare* (London: Oxford University Press, 1909), pp. 66-67.

anachronisms (with which Shakespeare's dramas abound) did not injure the possibility of illusion in the sixteenth century and the seventeenth, but in our time it is no longer possible to follow with interest the development of events which one knows could not take place in the conditions which the author describes in detail. . . .[3]

On the other hand, George Orwell in his essay, "Lear, Tolstoy, and the Fool," as a rebuttal to Tolstoy's indictment of Shakespeare's play, asserts that Tolstoy has given "the bare skeleton of the play," and has "cut out most of what is essential." The Fool, whom Tolstoy objects to as "simply a tedious nuisance and an excuse for making bad jokes," as well as the other characters that Tolstoy thought superfluous, is so conceived because of Tolstoy's narrow "range of human consciousness."

> . . .In Tolstoy's impatience with the Fool one gets a glimpse of his deeper quarrel with Shakespeare. He objects, with some justification, to the raggedness of Shakespeare's plays, the irrelevancies, the incredible plots, the exaggerated language: but what at bottom he probably most dislikes is a sort of exuberance, a tendency to take—not so much a pleasure, as simply an interest in the actual process of life. It is a mistake to write Tolstoy off as a moralist attacking an artist. He never said that art, as such, is wicked or meaningless, nor did he even say that technical virtuosity is unimportant. But his main aim, in later years, was to narrow the range of human consciousness. One's interests, one's points of attachment to the physical world and the day-to-day struggle, must be as few and not as many as possible. Literature must consist of parables, stripped of detail and almost independent of language . . . . Clearly, he could have no patience with a chaotic, detailed, discursive writer like Shakespeare . . . . Tolstoy does not know, perhaps, just *what* he misses in Shakespeare, but he is aware that he misses

---

[3]Leo Tolstoy, "On Shakespeare and the Drama," tr. V. Tchertkoff, *Fortnightly Review*, LXXXVI (1906), pp. 981-83.

something, and he 's determined that others shall
be deprived of it as well. . . .[4]

These comments not only illustrate the diversity of critical opinion but
demonstrate the contradictory and confusing nature of the play itself.
Without doubt, *King Lear* embraces in its structure incongruities,
inconsistencies, and thematic difficulties not found elsewhere in
Shakespearean drama. Unlike the worlds depicted in Shakespeare's
other plays, the complex *Lear* cosmos, as Bernard McElroy points out, is
"a violent, anarchic universe, wholly without a stable, inherent structure
and utterly devoid of meaning."[5]   Such a cosmos presents quandaries
bound to perplex those individuals within it by posing terrible questions
not only to them but also to us who behold their chaotic world.   McElroy
further maintains that Lear, as the protagonist and chief dramatic
spokesman in a world so divided and unstable that it has lost its moral
bearings, its social integrity, and all reliable dianoetic guidelines.

> . . . is forced to ask himself and the cosmos a
> series of questions, the answers to which hold
> terrible implications. If the hierarchy of state and
> family is not real, then what is? If he is not the
> king, then who or what is he? If the bonds of
> nature are not sanctioned by divine ordination,
> then what holds the world together?   If the
> trappings of civilization are superfluous
> "lendings," then what differentiates man from the
> animals? If the heavens are indifferent, if they do
> not love old men, if their sweet sway does not
> allow—*demand*—obedience, if they themselves
> are not old except in the myths of a collective
> imagination, if they do not send down and take the
> part of outraged kings and wronged fathers, then
> what becomes of justice and morality? If kingship
> itself is not a divinely established office, then what
> is the great image of authority?[6]

The agitation of the *Lear* universe with its violent disruption and its
wrenching of the moral platitudes and conventions of society is
appropriately congruent with the critical perplexities left in its wake.
Hard-pressed critics, staunchly aligning themselves against adversaries

---

[4]George Orwell, "Lea , Tolstoy, and the Fool," *Shooting an Elephant and other
Essays* (New York: Harcourt Brace and Co., 1959), pp. 41-42.

[5]Bernard McElroy, *Shakespeare's Mature Tragedies* (Princeton: Princeton
University Press, 1973), p. 145.

[6]McElroy, *Shakespeare's Mature Tragedies,* pp. 145-46.

equally adamant, commence furious scholarly warfare, the eventual outcome of which is usually an armistice; seldom does a decisive victor emerge.

Typical of the conflicts waged by critics regarding the intended import of the play is the thematic controversy about whether *King Lear* is a "Christian" play with optimistic overtones or a pessimistic "pagan" play affording little or no hope for man in a relentlessly indifferent world.[7] Among those scholars who have stressed the play's Christian implications is Roy W. Battenhouse. His views, in fact, extend beyond the number of Christian analogues that he detects in *King Lear* to conceive the drama as archetypically suggesting the whole history of the Hebraic religious heritage. Battenhouse considers that the change that comes over Gloucester after his "leap into self-abandonment" has allowed him "to discover . . . the strange reality of a good earth under him and a cheerful neighbor ready to befriend him" as simply a prelude to other spiritual episodes that contribute to Gloucester's "re-education."[8] One such important episode, according to Battenhouse, is the blind earl's meeting with the mad king, an encounter which cures Gloucester of self-pity as he grieves over Lear's misery. Gloucester's spiritual regeneration is plausible enough, but one's credulity is strained a bit at some of Battenhouse's highly fanciful interpretations, such as the following:

> A Gentleman leading [a search party for Lear] speaks of a daughter who "redeems nature from the general curse/ Which twain have brought." The "twain" here referred to are Goneril and Regan. Yet the whole phrase has an abstractness which echoes at another level too. It was Danby, I believe, who first suggested that Shakespeare at this intended his audience to be reminded of Adam and Eve, those "twain" ingrates of biblical story who brought on nature its first general curse. This archetypal level of suggestiveness may extend, I think, to other aspects of Lear's story as

---

[7]For a pithy abstract of the critical warfare over the "Christian" element in *King Lear,* see William R. Elton's *King Lear and the Gods* (San Marino, Calif.: Huntington Library Publications, 1965), pp. 3-8. For a fuller view of this controversy and for Elton's "refutation" of the Christian apologists and his contention that the play, "despite its Christian allusions, is more directly a syncretically pagan tragedy," read the whole book. Ably defending the Christian reading of the play while plausibly, if not always effectually, rebutting Elton's perspective is Herbert R. Coursen, Jr.'s *Christian Ritual and the World of Shakespeare's Tragedies* (Cranbury, N.J.: Associated University Presses, Inc., 1976), pp. 237-313.

[8]Roy W. Battenhouse, *Shakespearean Tragedy: Its Art and its Christian Premises* (Bloomington, Ind.: Indiana University Press, 1969), p. 271.

well. Let us recall that in Genesis, after the
twainness of Adam and Eve in their joint cupidity,
there follows an envy by Cain toward his brother,
then later a general depravity of human nature
which evokes a punishing flood from heaven, and
still later an ambition for self-glory which ends in a
Babel of tongues—four stages, all told, in the saga
of evil's spreading curse. Does not each of these
echo as a motif in Shakespeare's drama? For
example, in Act III we find introduced a rainstorm
which Lear interprets as a punishing flood, and
afterwards there are scenes in which Lear's
language breaks down into a babble of madtalk.
There had been no such episodes in any earlier
version of the Lear legend. One reason for
Shakespeare's inventing them may have been to
provide significant climax to the curse which is
befalling Lear. Under this curse we see Lear
flounder, an exile and a wanderer, until a rejected
child of his takes on a role analogous to that of a
Suffering Servant—and thus intervenes for the
healing of the spiritual illness of a father who has
come to epitomize, figuratively, St. Paul's concept
of the "old man."[9]

Though most recent commentators seem more optimistic than their
predecessors about the play's thematic conclusions, yet a significant
number of contemporary critics quarrel with contentions that this tragedy
conveys a sense of divine providence and order; that its protagonists
attain patience, humility, and regeneration through their sufferings; and
that the final impression is consistent with natural law and eternal justice.
Besides Elton's aforementioned views, D. J. James, F. P. Wilson, Arthur
Sewell, and Jan Kott have questioned or objected to the consolatory
interpretations that presently prevail, probably because of the anagogic
or the teleological predispositions derived from Christian indoctrination.
As Bernard McElroy has so cogently observed:

> . . . only in the case of Lear is criticism so sharply
> divided between an interpretation which sees it as
> the most glorious and transcendent dream of
> human redemption ever conceived, and one that
> sees it as the most unstintingly pessimistic

---

[9]Battenhouse, Shakespearean Tragedy: Its Art and Its Christian Premises, pp. 271-272.

indictment of the absurd human condition ever written.[10]

Clearly, a careful reader of *King Lear* must inevitably be struck by the gratuitous intrusion of incidents, characters, thematic discrepancies, anachronisms, and even *formal* aberrancies that preclude his regarding *Lear* from the wonted tragic perspective. The absurd anguish of both protagonists and the multiple incongruities that blatantly contradict the conventions of classical or even Elizabethan tragedy require a unique dramatic approach. Furthermore, the confusion of generic elements alien to conventional tragedy militates that one either dispense with orthodox views concerning the nature of tragedy or else re-define the genre if he is to regard *Lear* as such. For the play abounds with absurdities that tend to provoke mirth rather than pathos. The actions of both Lear and Gloucester, motivated as they are by stupid misapprehensions and ludicrously subjective judgments, afford ample humor, if the spectator could divest himself of sympathy or compassion for the pathetic protagonists. Indeed, it is probable that a totally objective reader or viewer of the drama, if he were unapprized of the fact that the play is supposed to be a tragedy, would regard a considerable part of its action as essentially comical. This comical action culminates when the two pathetic protagonists—the disoriented Lear and the blind, bumbling Gloucester—meet in that masterfully ironic sixth scene of Act IV. Here is what almost amounts to farce, if "impertinency" were not mixed with "matter" of primal importance. This scene, indeed, epitomizes almost the entire range of comic capability by extracting spiritual nutrition from a farcical situation while it achieves a fusion of feeling and knowledge; it cogently enforces C. L. Barber's dictum that typical Shakespearean comedy moves "through release to clarification."[11]

If, as Aristotle asserts, comedy "aims at representing man as worse, tragedy as better than in actual life,"[12] then one cannot deny to *King Lear* the comic perspective, for the play abounds in examples of human behavior below the norm, crass stupidities, and absurd misapprehensions of reality. The concept of comedy, unfortunately, is barely touched upon in Aristotle's *Poetics* . The philosopher does not elaborate upon what he understands by a man who is "worse" or one who is "better" than those in actual life. But I suspect that he intends by a "better" kind of man one who expresses or realizes qualities that dignify

---

[10]McElroy, *Shakespeare's Mature Tragedies,* p. 161.

[11]See C. L. Barber's *Shakespeare's Festive Comedy: A Study of Dramatic Form and Its Relation to Social Custom* (Princeton, 1959) and Northrop Frye's "The Mythos of Spring: Comedy" in *The Anatomy of Criticism* (Princeton University Press, 1957), pp. 163-186.

[12]Aristotle, *Poetics,* tr. S. H. Butcher (New York: Hill & Wang, 1961), p. 52.

the human estate and that indicate man's potential greatness or perhaps his incipient divinity. The "worse" kind of man, to whom comic treatment is befitting, would conversely express qualities never rising above what is conventional—qualities *common* to all human beings. Harold H. Watts aptly descibes the "modesty" that characterizes the comic playwright. According to Watts:

> . . . The comic writer may not leave the market-place; to ascend the hill, to address Capitoline Jove in eternal accents is not permitted him. His modesty constrains him from making assertions that the tragic poet *must* make if, indeed, he is to be a tragic poet. The tragic poet supposes that he sees truly and profoundly as concerns the will of the gods, human greatness and vileness, and the ties that link man with man. The tragic poet reports little or nothing of how people dress and amuse themselves, how they make their living, and how they consult one soothsayer after another. Not his concern is man's stubborn refusal to understand his fellows—and, for that matter, his even more stubborn timidity which keeps him from pushing to bloody extremes the results of his misunderstanding. These things lie in the province of the comic writer.[13]

Although Watts properly perceives, as did Aristotle before him, that the comic focus centers on the mundane, prosaic, and common aspects of human life, nor presumes to treat issues privately reserved for the tragic sensibility; yet neither Watts nor Aristotle remarks that the conception of the "great " man and the "lesser" man varies from one society to the next; nor does either critic sufficiently stress that one man's "greatness" or "littleness" is relative to the conventions and norms of the society regarding him. The fact is that both the tragic and the comic sense of life appear only when an individual is perceived to violate the prevailing social norms. As long as one is thought to be "in step" with what society condones, considers proper, or even holds sacrosanct, there is no perception of either tragedy or comedy. The "normal" man, however uninteresting he may be, is one whose behavior conforms to social decorum and convention; as long as he remains "normal," his actions elicit neither a tragic nor a comic response from an audience subject to the same norms.

---

[13]Harold H. Watts, "The Sense of Regain: A Theory of Comedy," *University of Kansas City Review,* Vol. xiii, No. 1 (Autumn, 1946), pp. 19-20.

The apparent distinction generally made between comedy and tragedy primarily rests upon the conventions of a particular society. A breach of those conventions, when it is neither injurious nor seemingly intentional, produces a comic response. This response proceeds from the recognition of inadequacy or failure in an individual to "measure up" to society's norms or expectations. The failure to "measure up" is caused by some incompetence, inability, or ignorance in a person whose efforts to conform are unsuccessful. This person is Aristotle's "inferior" man who, because of some physical, moral, or intellectual infirmity, is unable to make his behavior congruent with the norms of society. He earnestly tries to "measure up," but cannot; he is therefore laughed at, but forgiven, because his violation of conventional behavioral standards is neither malicious nor intentional. Laughter is the usual response to his abnormalities and absurdities, because his incongruous behavior poses no threat to the institutions and conventions upheld by that society. Because he is innocuous, at least not a danger to society, he is regarded as comical, and self-congratulatory laughter is the normal reponse to his ineffectual attempts to function well in his society.

The tragic sense also arises from a violation of society's norms. But the tragic individual is not one who is unable to "measure up" because of a personal incapacity or ineptitude; rather, he is one who has the ability to conform acceptably to social dictates but does not. He is tragic because social norms are beneath him; they are not worthy of him, but they constrain behavior which insults his superior capabilities and conceptions. The norms to which his society subscribes are debilitating impediments to his self-fulfillment; he feels crippled and imposed upon by these normative constraints. The very conventions which provide security and a sense of well-being to the "normal" people in a society are the habits and rituals that inhibit his development as an individual; he, therefore, in transcending them seems to contradict the "sacred cows" that succour the mass of men in his society. His "superiority," as Aristotle calls it, disables him from normative behavior, just as the "inferior" man is disabled therefrom by ineptitude. But because he is beyond its norms, the behavior of the "tragic" man poses a threat to society; for he "sees through" convention and does not try to "measure up." Therefore, the reaction of an audience in viewing tragedy, as Aristotle points out, is pity and fear. The audience feels pity because it recognizes the excellence, the "superiority," of the protagonist, and it feels fear because it recognizes also the threat posed to society's norms and religious beliefs by such an individual. The emotions of the audience are aroused by the tragic protagonist because it feels that his probings into reality seriously question its ritualistic practice and threaten its values and religious posture. Consciously or unconsciously, the audience senses that the dilemma of the tragic protagonist is essentially the dilemma faced by all men, if they were also "exceptional" enough to front reality.

The comic audience, on the other hand, feels no such anxiety or pity, because its emotions are not engaged by the petty dilemmas of the "inferior" protagonist. Since his indiscretions, his absurdities, pose no real threat to the social structure, his actions are "judged" intellectually; for the "normal" audience can easily gauge the behavior of a "subnormal" protagonist. The comic protagonist, then, elicits an intellectual response rather than an emotional one, for the audience does not take his abnormal or unconventional behavior seriously; there is no threat to its own security.

Of course, the conventions of societies differ; even the norms of a single given society change through the years. Consequently, what is tragic or comic to one generation might not be so to previous or to subsequent generations. The truth is that the appreciation of either tragedy or comedy requires that an audience at least understand, if it cannot reappropriate nor identify with, the norms of the society that spawned the dramatic spectacle being performed. A dramatic performance is always translated into the social idiom of its audience, and if its audience does not share the values and the conventions that govern the action of the play, then the intended effect of the play is nullified. This dependence of dramatic effect upon the audience's societally induced predisposition obviously arbitrates the tragic or cosmic impact that the play accomplishes and therefore generically modifies the drama itself. As a result, one should bear in mind that a play originally intended as tragedy might with the passage of time be translated into melodrama or even comedy, if the values of the audience's society differ drastically from the conventions and values entertained by the characters in the drama. The *objective* generic form of the play (the genre intended by its author) is frequently modified by the *subjective* form supplied by the audience's interpretation.

Furthermore, even when the tragic and comic terminology remains, the conception of each is radically altered. In a society such as ours, where *qualitative* values have all but evaporated and where *quantitative* criteria determine worth, the tragic conception of life has been supplanted by sheer violence and aggregated misery—both unredeemed by any concomitant human amelioration and advancement or by any intimation that the human condition, either intrinsically or potentially, has dignity or value. Comedy today has relapsed into a farcical repetition of absurdities and improbabilities—the massive accumulation of which provokes an indiscriminate, non-critical mirth which fails to engender any positive attitudes toward value nor any definite social consequences—none at least that are ameliorative.

10

In the light of the contemporary disintegration of values, it seems almost inpertinent to retain the separate conceptions of life represented by tragedy and comedy. Robert Corrigan has pointed out that

> . . .One of the most striking characteristics of the modern drama is the way in which the age-old distinctions between the tragic and the comic (the serious and the ludicrous, the painful and the painless) have been obliterated. This has not been a process of commingling as so many critics have, I believe, erroneously asserted. . . . But what is happening today is something quite different. So much so, that it is questionable whether we should even use the terms comedy and tragedy any longer.[14]

Clearly, the lines of demarcation that separate the comic genre from the tragic are tenuous and perhaps even arbitrary. Neither form can exist unless there are norms and values that a society sustains and takes seriously. When normative values and conventions dissipate or break down, both the comic and tragic viewpoints become at first confused, then almost indistinguishable. Again, Corrigan pertinently diagnoses what has occurred in modern drama:

> . . . both tragedy and comedy depend upon generally accepted standards of values. Such norms make it possible to establish those hierarchies of seriousness upon which the drama has been traditionally based. However, because in our time Nietzsche shouted, "God is dead!" there are no generally accepted values, no universally valid systems, no publicly meaningful hierarchies. Without them all experience becomes equally serious or equally ludicrous. Or, as Ionesco said, "It all comes to the same thing anyway: comic and tragic are merely two aspects of the same situation, and I have now reached the stage when I find it hard to distinguish one from the other."[15]

The action in *King Lear,* if not symptomatic of a world in collapse, at least attests the moribundity of that world's values. It is a divided world,

---

[14]Robert W. Corrigan, *Comedy: Meaning and Form* (San Francisco: Chandler Publishing Co., 1965), p. 9.
[15]*Ibid.*

much like our own, with "generation gaps," pointless wanderings over "barren heaths," personal insecurity, and incertitude about one's status in a "kingless" kingdom. It is a realm whose rulers exercise a dubious authority, yet hold sway while either ignoring or abusing the conventions and social rituals that provide political stability and meaning. In such a world, the boundaries between the serious and the trivial evaporate. In Shakespeare's other major dramas, the comic and tragic strands are distinguishable from, though often complementary to, each other; but in the *Lear* universe, the two are inseparably blent, so that their individual identities are lost, or, I would say, that they are married or rebaptized in the name of "irony."

At any rate, the comic elements in *King Lear* seem as instrumental to its action as the more serious concerns. Lear himself is not "exceptional" in the sense that Hamlet, Othello, or Macbeth is. In fact, if he did not enjoy regality of station, he would perhaps be a character more suitable for comedy than tragedy. Certainly both he and Gloucester lack the "superiority" that Aristotle ascribes to the tragic protagonist; neither are imposed upon by social convention or customs that inhibit self-development. Rather, they are enabled by their high offices to wrench convention to their own self-service. Lear distends the paternal-filial bond to allow exorbitant love from his daughters; Gloucester abuses the institution of marriage by violating the conjugal love bond to gratify his desire for illicit sexuality.

Although some of Lear's utterances are among the most heart-rendingly pathetic in all literature, they are not far removed from comedy when one considers the ridiculous acts that prompt them. Consider, for example, Lear's terrible judgments on Cordelia and Kent. Such judgments, coming from a king, are serious enough, but they arise from Lear's faulty discernment and his excessive self-esteem; and a primary source of comedy is one's mistaking appearances for reality or one's treating trivialities too seriously. The causes of Kent's and Cordelia's banishments, though trivial, give rise to tragic effects. That one who "hath ever but slenderly known himself,"[16] wields such power is ludicrous. That a man so ill-qualified to pass judgment is vested with such absolute judicial power seems absurd. Furthermore, the serious formality that attends Lear's abdication and the conferring of his authority and his realm upon his daughters seems incongruous with the ridiculous criterion used to ascertain their fitness for such power.

---

[16]"King Lear," *The Complete Works of Shakespeare,* ed. by George L. Kittredge (Boston: Ginn and Company, 1936), 1, i, 11. 296-7. Subsequent references to *King Lear* are indicated by identification of acts, scenes, and lines, parenthetically inserted into this text.

Such apparently incongruous, scarcely credible circumstances and events certainly appear unlikely to produce a sense of reality. But they are, nevertheless, quite consistent with the play's mythic tone; and *Lear*, somewhat like a fairy tale, by its implementation of primitive forces and its stripping away the encrusted bark of civilization, exposes to its audience the very tree of life—the archetypal experience of collective man. As F. D. Hoeniger has observed, "The utterly unreal becomes profoundly real."[17]

In the lengthy first scene of the play, Shakespeare makes it clear that his two central characters, Lear and Gloucester, though men of authority, irresponsibly defer to their feelings and therefore mishandle their administrative functions. They grievously misconceive themselves, other people, and the circumstances of life and society. Gloucester, in his initial conversation with Kent, grossly gloats about his bastard son Edmund and with licentious levity refers to the "good sport at his making." (I, i, 23-24) Because he sees with his feelings and has blunted his moral sensibilities, Gloucester has exempted himself from the familial bonds that supply social integrity. By violating the sanctity of the home, he has spawned a bastard who is destined to undermine and eventually supplant him. Gloucester's sensual malfeasances correlate to Lear's mental indiscretions; it is, in fact, apparent that Gloucester's corporeality is the physical counterpart of Lear's mentality. Upon these two central figures the other characters depend. But though Lear and Gloucester are the fathers of, or the sources of being for, the other characters, their authority, vitiated as it is by their subjectivity, misconstrues both itself and the true nature of those who depend upon it. As a result, both protagonists favor and embrace the vicious and alienate or banish the virtuous characters. Gloucester dotes on Edmund and rejects Edgar; Lear favors Burgundy rather than France, prefers Goneril and Regan to Cordelia, and banishes Kent, his honest monitor. The grounds for Lear's and Gloucester's judgments are based upon these protagonists' superficial, subjective appraisals of reality and upon their grossly overweening self-esteem. But incongruously serious calamity is the consequence of their absurdly subjective judgments.

Throughout the play trivial incidents and minor offenses result in terrible consequences. Edgar is banished on merely circumstantial evidence; Kent is put into the stocks for rudeness to Oswald and Cornwall, a severe punishment for so small an offense; and Gloucester's eyes are put out simply to gratify the cruelty of Regan and Cornwall. The

[17]See F. D. Hoeniger's "The Artist Exploring the Primitive: *King Lear*," an essay appearing in Rosalie Colie's and F. T. Flahiff's *Some Facets of 'King Lear' : Essays in Prismatic Criticism* (Toronto: University of Toronto Press, 1974), pp. 89-102. By showing that the *Lear* story is 'primitive in setting. . . [and] in origin,' Hoeniger agrees with Maynard Mack 'that the play has many archetypal elements of a folktale. . . .'

play abounds with such incongruities of cause and effect. Even Lear's grand apostrophes are generally excited by matters of a trivial nature. Although his tirade against the winds and rain (III, ii, 1-24) is magnificent, his splenetic eloquence is wasted, absurdly enough, upon the foul weather, about which he is powerless to do anything. Though his speech is impassioned and pathetic, one can hardly restrain laughter when one reflects upon the absurdity of a man's vehement outcry against the indifferent and unresponding elements. The insane Lear's meeting with the blind Gloucester (IV, vi) is also quite heart-rending; yet in the interchange of words between the two, one notes with Edgar "matter and impertinency mix'd." The effect is not altogether tragic, but comic too. Consider also that Lear's terrible maledictions upon Regan and Goneril are unseemly pronouncements for a father to invoke upon his children. Even the fact that father and child are at deadly odds with each other is another incongruity, which is rightly treated with profound seriousness.

Despite his agonies and the sympathy aroused by them, Gloucester is likewise comical if one views the absurd basis for most of his judgments. It is absurd that he should so rashly act upon Edmund's venomous implications of Edgar's treachery. Gloucester, after all, has not seen Edmund for nine years (I, i, 33) , whereas Edgar appears to have been in his father's castle during this whole time. Surely, the old man ought to be able to gauge more accurately Edgar's character than he does. Further, it strikes one as odd that he does not know Edgar's handwriting (I, ii, 66). Why, as a matter of fact, does Edgar supposedly write a letter to Edmund instead of speaking with him? Both apparently reside in the same household. Finally, is it not ludicrous that Gloucester so quickly concludes that Edgar deserves immediate death upon his capture? Apparently Gloucester does not intend to allow Edgar to offer any testimony in his own behalf, but intends to execute him summarily without trial (II, i, 58-65). It is also rather amusing to speculate about the reasons for Gloucester's journeying to Dover in order to commit suicide. The attempted suicide itself is ludicrous to the objective observer, though, of course, quite pathetic to Edgar or to anyone else who is sympathetic to Gloucester. It is absurd, as well as pathetic, that Gloucester, like Lear, seems always to believe those persons who are most malevolent toward him. Lear believes Goneril and Regan and prefers Burgundy to France; Gloucester believes Edmund, crediting his loyalty rather than Edgar's, and holds Cornwall in high esteem.

If, as Aristotle maintains, the tragic protagonist is a character of a high estate, how can such incredulous asses as Lear and Gloucester be worthy of tragic treatment? If tragedy dramatizes the serious rather than the ludicrous, how can one call *King Lear* a tragedy, when the ludicrous and the serious are inseparably knit? If in tragedy pity is supposed to be aroused by unmerited misfortune, how can this play be classified as tragedy, since both protagonists, by their own demerits, implement their misfortunes? And there is certainly some doubt as to Shakespeare's presenting men in this play as being better than those in actual life. Certainly it appears that *King Lear* is *not* a tragedy, if judged by Aristotelian standards.

And yet, despite the comic intrusions and the departures from classical tradition, the drama achieves and perhaps intensifies many tragic effects. If *King Lear* is not truly a tragedy, it nevertheless seems the culmination of a dramatic form toward which Shakespeare had been tending in his earlier tragedies. Most of his previous dramas had made use of swiftly alternating scenes of tragedy and tomfoolery. As Boris Pasternak remarks,

> On the edge of Ophelia's grave the audience is made to laugh at the philosophizing of the gravediggers. At the moment when Juliet's corpse is carried out, the boy from the servants' hall giggles at the musicians who have been invited to a wedding, and the musicians bargain with the nurse, who is trying to get rid of them. Cleopatra's suicide is preceded by the appearance of the half-wit Egyptian snake-charmer with his absurd reflections on the uselessness of reptiles—almost as in Maeterlinck or in Leonid Andretev![18]

These are but a few of the many scenes by which Shakespeare heightens the sense of tragedy by introducing comedy in its midst. One might add from a host of other examples the drunken porter scene immediately following Macbeth's murder of Duncan. But Shakespeare in *King Lear* is not merely heightening the tragic effect by inserting comedy amid tragic incidents; he is pointing up an essential truth of human existence. Tragedy and comedy are not mutually exclusive, but are instead essential to each other; they are intrinsic threads making up the fabric of life. In *King Lear* comic scenes are not added in order to heighten the tragic effect, as is the case in most other tragedies, but are instead *blended* with the serious action; the result is a dramatic effect at once serious and ludicrous, or, in a word, *ironic.* Tragedy and comedy are the strands out of which is woven the fabric of the *Lear* universe. By blending tragedy and comedy as the constituent essentials of the play, I believe that Shakespeare has portrayed the human dilemma with more fidelity than is possible by focusing on man's life from either the tragic or the comic perspective. To separate tragedy from comedy, or vice versa,

---

[18]Boris Pasternak, *I Remember* (New York: Pantheon Books Inc., 1959), pp. 148-49.

is to present a biased or one-sided view of human life, for man's life is not merely tragic nor merely comic, but both at once. Shakespeare's preeminence as a playwright may well be the result of his realization that tragedy and comedy are simply aspectual components of human life and that the most effective representation of either requires mastery of both points of view.

But to observe that the blending of serious and comic elements accounts in part for many incongruities in the play does not, of course, cut Shakespeare's Gordian knot nor resolve the perplexities troubling redoubtable scholars; not does it adequately address other complexities and alleged superfluities that have offended readers like Bradley, Tolstoy, and Murry. To regard *King Lear* merely as a play compounded of tragic and comic elements indistinguishably melted together is to over-simplify the rich complexity of the drama. Shakespeare, it seems to me, has not merely reconciled tragedy and comedy, but he has amalgamated all the notable dramatic genres familiar to Elizabethan playwrights. He has effected in *King Lear* a comprehensive dramatic form that harmonizes and unifies all the divergent dramatic tendencies of his age. *King Lear,* in fact, comprises the tragic, comic, chronicle, morality, and miracle dramatic traditions. Shakespeare, perhaps disenchanted by, or at least dissatisfied with, the limited views of life presented by each of the conventional dramatic types, has indissolubly knit all these traditions and formed a composite drama which deals with the manifold complexities of life. Each conventional dramatic form concentrates upon a single aspect of man's nature: tragedy emphasizes the nobility and pathos of man's predicament; comedy concentrates upon man's absurdity; the chronicle deals with the deeds and historical accomplishments of man; the morality plays and the miracle plays accentuate man's moral nature and his religious proclivities. Each offers at best only a one-sided view of man; they deal only with aspects of the human predicament. But the human situation is far more complex than any one of these types of drama can depict. The whole nature of man comprises all the functions and faculties separately emphasized by each of these dramatic types. Tragedy appeals primarily to the emotions, comedy to the intellect, the moralities and miracle play to the spirit, and the chronicles to man's sense of accomplishment; but in reality, no man's life can be wholly summarized by its pathos, its comedy, its spirituality, or its works. A complete view of human life must include all facets of man's being: *King Lear* attempts this comprehensive view of the human predicament. In accordance with the Renaissance belief that personal wholeness requires a well-integrated personality, one in which all the human faculties—intellect, will, emotions—are adequately developed and harmonized, *King Lear* attempts to achieve concomitant dramatic integrity by supplying the most comprehensive view of man that exists in our literature. For *King Lear* provides not merely a partial view of the human dilemma, but treats of human life in its multiple aspects.

Portraying the whole man, it does not leave a dominant impression of man's futility, or his pathos, or his spirituality, or his greatness; man is shown as he is. He *is* inept, pathetic, absurd, spiritual, and great; but he is all these at the same time. His predicament, because of its aberrancies, contradictions, and inconsistencies, is essentially ironic. Instead of a tragic conception of man, the play ultimately impresses us with the ironic nature of human life.

My primary intention now is to demonstrate the superiority of ironical drama to tragedy and to show that *King Lear*, more adequately than any precedent drama, attests this fact. Whereas other dramas had utilized irony to point up tragedy or comedy, *King Lear* employs comedy and tragedy to point up irony. A résumé of analyses of irony leading to a definition of techniques observable in *King Lear* should enable one, through a subsequent analysis of the play, to appreciate Shakespeare's achievement. But first, it will be necessary to elaborate why *King Lear* cannot accurately be called a tragedy.

CHAPTER II

KING LEAR AS AN ANTI-CLASSICAL TRAGEDY

If, in fact, *King Lear* is not a true tragedy, what sort of drama is it? A few of the comic elements upon which much of the serious action depends have been pointed out as an initial inquiry into the real nature of the play. As yet, however, no definitive attempt has been made to classify it as a distinct dramatic genre. Before such a classification can be made, it is necessary to demonstrate its deficiencies as a tragedy. To disclaim the appropriateness of the designation it bears in no way detracts from its reputation as an untimately serious and lofty drama; for, even though it flagrantly violates the requisites for conventional tragedy, its impact certainly equals, perhaps even exceeds, the magnitude and seriousness of tragedy.

In order to clarify and evaluate Shakespeare's dramatic intentions and accomplishments in *King Lear*, it will be necessary to consider initially the classical conception of tragedy as defined by Aristotle's *Poetics*. During the fifteenth and sixteenth centuries, English university scholastics and humanists had attacked contemporary tragedy, especially deploring its structural laxity, its sensational qualities, and its comic intrusions, as well as other improprieties.[19] Even though English drama had largely evolved independently of classical influences, yet Aristotle's tragical contentions were still considered almost sacrosanct by most Elizabethan scholastics. The dramatic models that Elizabethan playwrights had found most amenable to their own purposes were those of Seneca and Plautus, but these dramatists, unfortunately, were also frequently out of step with Aristotle. As a result, though in practice English drama was well received, on critical grounds it seemed virtually indefensible. The*Poetics*, after all, offered the only definitive treatment of tragedy available to the Elizabethan playwrights.

Of the six formative elements of tragedy described in the *Poetics*—spectacle, character, plot (fable), diction, song, and thought—plot is considered primary by Aristotle.

---

[19]O. B. Hardison, Jr.'s "Logic Versus the Slovenly World in Shakespearean Comedy," *Shakespeare Quarterly* XXXI:3 (1980), 311 ff., throws light upon the generic ambiguities of English drama during the Renaissance. Hardison states that the scholastic quandary engendered by Shakespearean drama resulted in 'critical schizophrenia' for at least two centuries.

The Plot, then, is the first principle, and, as it were, the soul of a tragedy: Character holds the second place. A similar fact is seen in painting. The most beautiful colors, laid on confusedly, will not give as much pleasure as the chalk outline of a portrait. Thus tragedy is the imitation of an action, and of the agents mainly with a view to the action.[20]

But in *King Lear,* Shakespeare places more emphasis upon the characters than upon plot. It is not so much what Lear and Gloucester do that elicits our most serious attention; what they do is, in fact, often rather ludicrous. Who they are, rather than what they do, evokes the sympathy of the spectator. Were they not men in high place, men of authority, their actions would seldom call forth serious concern. A. C. Bradley has pointed out that Shakespeare seems little concerned about the actions of the men; he is careless in his elaboration of incident in the play, and the two plots are integrated in a rather slipshod, somewhat unrealistic way. But the actions of the two protagonists are merely symptomatic manifestations of their natures. Maynard Mack, noting that the plot in *King Lear* provides scanty motivation for most of the characters in the play, remarks the dominance of "psychic life" over the "fluctuating motives" provided by the action.[21] Whatever pathos is aroused in the discerning spectator is elicited not so much by the play's action as by the identification of himself with the characters. This emphasis upon character is nothing new in Shakespearean drama, but in *King Lear* the shift from plot to character is certainly more radical than elsewhere. For the action itself, as has been pointed out, derives from rather absurd antecedents and would evoke little more than laughter, were it not understood and appreciated in terms of the characters responsible for the action.

Already I have shown that Lear and Gloucester are not superior men, an Aristotelian requisite for tragic protagonists. Aristotle would have considered neither of them worthy of tragic treatment. Alan Hobson even goes so far as to deny Lear maturity, claiming that his egocentricity reflects the selfishness typical of an infant who lacks the capacity for making deliberate choices.

> . . .Maturation is thus growth in relationship, a progress to altruism. Maturity, in this sense, is never reached. . . .

---

[20]Aristotle, *Poetics,* p. 63.

[21]Maynard Mack, *King Lear in Our Time* (Berkeley and Los Angeles: University of California Press, 1965), p. 66.

King Lear, 'fourscore and upward,' remains a great baby, but a ranting, towering very dangerous baby. He is also a mighty king, majestic and terrible. . . . 'The best and soundest of his time has been but rash,' and, now, in the division of the kingdom, he is moved by violent impulse and childish vanity. The startling naivety of his plan to divide the kingdom into three for his three daughters 'that future strife may be prevented now', but not into three equal parts (for he is not impartial: Cordelia is his joy and he thinks to set his rest 'on her kind nursery')—such naivety is credible only in dotage, or in one whose course of royalty has run smooth and whom there has been none to gainsay. The same naivety accompanies the childish vanity which, not content with the love of a true daughter, will have that love displayed in open court for all to see, and yet so disposes as to choke and curb true love and give the rein to flattery and falsehood: . . .[22]

Shakespeare has in *King Lear* inverted the classical tradition of representing a protagonist who is superior to the mass of men by substituting one who is ordinary—perhaps in some respects subordinary. Furthermore, instead of having *one* protagonist, Shakespeare has *two* ! And the tragic isolation of each is not wrought in the conventional manner. Ordinarily the protagonist is isolated from others because of his superiority. Lear's and Gloucester's isolation, however, does not result from the failure of others to understand them, but it is brought about by their inability to understand or sympathize with others. Although their isolation is not therefore less real, it is accomplished in a manner opposite to the conventional. In addition, the tragic protagonist usually is manifestly tragic. Such, however, is not the case in *King Lear*. Only by regarding the protagonists as they regard themselves can one truly view them as tragic figures, for their tragedies are *subjective* rather than *objective*. Though they conceive themselves and their predicaments as tragic, one, unless he identifies with them, cannot conceive them in that light.

Another element that Aristotle regarded as essential to classical tragedy is song. For the main part, song in Greek tragedy is provided by a chorus. The chorus usually is omitted in the tragedies of the English Renaissance, though frequently the comedies and chronicle plays of the period employ a "chorus" (usually one person) to introduce a play or as prologue to the several Acts of drama and for the epilogue at its

---

[22]Alan Hobson, Full Circle: *Shakespeare and Moral Development* (New York: Barnes & Noble, Inc. 1972), p. 15.

conclusion. Music and songs are regularly featured in almost all Elizabethan dramas, but a chorus of twelve or fifteen is very seldom, if ever, utilized in English drama as it was in Greek tragedy. In *King Lear,* music is used as therapy for Lear's madness, and songs are sometimes sung by the Fool when he attends upon Lear. But the music and song in *Lear,* as is often the case with English drama of the Renaissance, serve a different purpose than in Greek tragedy. G. Wilson Knight describes the therapeutic function of music when Lear, recuperating from his madness, is sleeping in a tent at the French camp:

> Music and love; replacing for awhile tempest and mental agony, the music of a daughter's love to heal the harsh unmusic of madness. . . .Sleep, music, nature's simples and Cordelia's love are the Doctor's medicines. Now the doctor would have him wake; 'Louder the music there!' (IV.vii.25). Cordelia kisses him, speaks those lines we have just quoted recalling the tempest, so that recollection of that tempest is now divinely enclosed in music. Lear wakes, and is redeemed into sanity, love, peace. Again in *Lear* we have a powerful tempest-music opposition. Consider the Shakespearian sonnet where child and father and happy mother sing one note of family concord. That harmony is broken here in the first act; the 'tempest' of division, anguish, and madness ensues; then restoration is born for awhile on Cordelia's lips, and Lear wakes, as a mortal man to immortality, wakes into music and love.[23]

The songs and the music in Shakespearean drama, it is apparent, seldom conform to the purposes of choric song in Greek tragedy. In *Lear,* although Shakespeare does not altogether dispense with the chorus, if the Fool assumes that role, as many critics believe he does; it is obvious that the Fool, both in function and in form, differs radically from the traditional Greek chorus.[24]   In the first place, the Fool is one man instead of a group of men; second, the point of view expressed by him does not necessarily correspond to or reflect public opinion or the ideas

---

[23]G. Wilson Knight, *The Shakespearian Tempest* (London: Methuen & Co., 1953), pp. 198-199.

[24]The idea that the Fool functions in *King Lear* as a chorus seems to be generally held by Shakespearean scholars. Among many others who have so conceived him are John W. Draper in "The Occasion of *King Lear,"* *Studies in Philology,* XXXIV (1937), 179; W. H. Clemen in *The Development of Shakespeare's Imagery* (Cambridge, Mass.: Harvard University Press, 1951), 142; and George Lyman Kittredge in his Introduction to "King Lear" from the Kittredge edition of Shakespeare's *Works.*

of the author, nor does he provide information needed by the audience for comprehending the theme or action. Neither does he express himself in lyrical passages as does the Greek chorus. As a matter of fact, his speech is prosaic rather than lyrical, often enigmatically abounding in paradox, proverbs, and sometimes sheer nonsense. The Fool, unlike the Greek chorus, disappears suddenly from the play at the very height of its action; he is not present at the end of the drama nor during most of its crucial moments, as the Greek chorus invariably is. What he says does not heighten the climax of the crucial actions, but comes anticlimactically after a crisis has occurred.

In other words, the Fool's statements, unlike those of the Greek chorus, do not significantly contribute to nor intensify dramatic tautness, but instead relieve the tension already built up. As a consequence, the purpose he serves seems almost directly opposite to that achieved by the Greek chorus. For he functions not only as choric but also as Lear's alter ego in that he expresses what Lear's consciousness has not yet grasped; hence, when Lear becomes mad, The Fool, no longer able to communicate with him, disappears. To replace the Fool, Cordelia then reappears in the drama as the therapeutic agent that abets the purgative eradication of Lear's egocentricity.

Shakespeare's failure to observe the so-called tragic "Unities" of time, place and action constitutes no real violation of classical decorum, for Aristotle made no mention of the Unities in his *Poetics;* these are a later invention of the seventeenth century. But even the French neoclassical playwrights, to whom these Unities were most important, did not always preserve them. There is no question, however, that Shakespeare, more so than is usual in Elizabethan dramaturgy, is exceedingly negligent about time, place, and action. In *Lear*, the time certainly extends beyond the twenty-four hour limit characteristic of Greek tragedy. In fact, it is most difficult, if not impossible, to determine just how much time elapses from the beginning to the end of the play.[25] The customs, the admixture of Christian and paganistic allusions, the speech of the characters, the anachronisms so strenuously objected to by Tolstoy, the structure of the English state—all these co-existing elements contribute to such a sense of vagueness in time that one can as easily conceive of the action as occurring in the Middle Ages or during the Renaissance as he can imagine its happening in the pre-Christian era of English history.

The unity of place, characteristic of Greek tragedy though not an Aristotelian requirement, is flagrantly violated. A. C. Bradley quite

---

[25]See Mack, *King Lear in Our Time*, pp. 77-78. The intentional vagueness of Shakespeare in regard to both time and place is discussed here.

pertinently points out that one achieves a sense of vagueness regarding the actual locations for the action of *King Lear.*

> Nothing enables us to imagine whereabouts in Britain Lear's palace lies, or where the Duke of Albany lives. In referring to the dividing lines on the map, Lear tells us of shadowy forest and plenteous rivers, but. . .he studiously avoids proper names. The Duke of Cornwall, we presume in the absence of information, is likely to live in Cornwall; but we suddenly find, from the introduction of a place name which all readers take at first for a surname, that he lives at Gloster (I, v, 1). This seems likely to be also the home of the Earl of Gloster, to whom Cornwall is patron. But no: it is a night's journey from Cornwall's "house" to Gloster's, and Gloster's is in the middle of an uninhabited heath. Here, for the purpose of the crisis, nearly all the persons assemble, but they do so in a manner which no casual spectator or reader could follow. Afterwards they all drift towards Dover for the purpose of the catastrophe; but again the localities and movements are unusually indefinite. . . .[26]

Neither is the action in *King Lear* unified. Instead of focusing on one central action, as is customary in Greek tragedy, Shakespeare has supplied a double plot. Furthermore, both plots are episodic, a flaw Aristotle considers egregious.

> Of all plots and actions the epeisodic are the worst. I call a plot "epeisodic" in which the epeisodes or acts succeed one another without probable or necessary sequence. Bad poets compose such pieces by their own fault, good poets, to please the players; for, as they write show pieces for competition, they stretch the plot beyond its capacity and are often forced to break the natural continuity.[27]

That *King Lear* is episodic needs little proof. The Gloucester plot, itself not indispensable to the play as far as the primary action is concerned,

---

[26]A. C. Bradley, *Shakespearean Tragedy,* Second Edition (London: Macmillan and Co., Ltd., 1905), pp. 259-60.

[27]Aristotle, *Poetics,* p. 69.

24

chiefly intensifies and reinforces the theme, while, by arousing secondary interest, it alleviates the emotional impact of the Lear plot. Maynard Mack interestingly contends that the Gloucester plot's part in *King Lear* is

> . . .to extend and consummate the play's wide-ranging vision of the nature and destiny of man. On this account, though the subplot's line of action sometimes crosses and ev .n merges with tha ̇ of the main plot in an external way, the relation of the two plots remains homiletic rather than dramatic: Gloucester's story is never permitted to discharge its full energies into the consciousness of Lear. The expulsion of Edgar; the fact that it is Edgar whom Lear meets on the heath as the thing itself; Edmund's rise to power, his relation with Lear's daughters, and his eventual defeat; Gloucester's blinding, expulsion, attempted suicide, and happy ending—these are all events of tragic import as we see them in the theater, which come to Lear's attention only dimly (when they come at all) and make no part of his tragic experience. Their presence in the play is entirely dictated by their meaning for *us* .[28]

Whatever dramatic function one imputes to the subplot, the fact remains that a number of scenes in *King Lear* are not probable, necessary, or even sequential to the major incidents of the play. One such scene is the eye-gouging scene, which only augments the dislike already felt for Cornwall, Regan, Goneril, and Edmund. Another superfluous scene, dealing with Gloucester's attempted suicide, does little more than teach patience to Gloucester and make the spectator wonder at Edgar's deceiving his father. Certainly it is extremely improbable, despite Gloucester's credulity, that the blind Earl should be convinced that he is on the summit of a cliff and then be persuaded that he has jumped from this cliff and fallen a considerable distance without injury, when in reality he has only fallen forward. Many such incidents have little or no bearing upon the main action but simply divert or occasionally afford either insight into the natures of the characters or thematic illumination.

Shakespeare commits another flagrant violation of Greek convention when in *King Lear* he presents violence on stage. Again, though it is true that on-stage violence is the rule rather than an exception during the

---

[28]Mack, *King Lear in Our Time,* p. 71.

English Renaissance, in *King Lear* Shakespeare once more seems to flout the Greek tradition. The obvious parallel to Gloucester's blinding occurs in the Greek tragedy *Oedipus Tyrannus.* In both plays the protagonists' eyes are gouged out. But whereas Shakespeare presents this violent act on the stage, Sophocles has a messenger report the blinding of Oedipus. Obviously Shakespeare here has intentionally violated a Greek tragic convention. This occurrence corresponds too closely to the Oedipus incident to be accidental; it is apparent that Shakespeare willfully contradicts the traditional Greek attitude toward violence.

Let it furthermore be noted that Shakespearean tragedy seldom, if ever, achieves the same cathartic effect experienced in classical tragedy. Nor is it difficult to understand why. In Greek drama the tragic intensity disallows relaxation of the emotional strain built up by the excitation of pity and fear. Since its dramatic action centers upon a single central incident, there is permitted no tragic easement, no distracting secondary interest to relax the emotional intensity of the audience through comic by-play, moral discursiveness, or intellectual reflectivity. The play's focus, accordingly, is entirely upon the central character and his suffering. Such concentration upon one character and his anguish precludes relief from the emotional tension which classical tragedy aims at. Catharsis, therefore, is the natural and inevitable result of such drama, so that when the play concludes, the audience feels itself emotionally drained or purged by its impact.

But Shakespearean tragedy, while it also primarily addresses the dilemma and the suffering of the protagonist, additionally affords distraction from the anguish of the protagonist by intruding comic relief, intellectual distance from the emotional taxation exacted by the suffering hero, and objective correlatives to the play's tragic bias. This dispersal of the tragic focus provides dramatic amplitude to Shakespeare's audience. Furthermore, by breaking up the emotional light, which in Greek tragedy is solely concentrated on the protagonist, Shakespeare enables the other characters prismatically to reflect and convey multiple facets of the protagonist's essential anguish. Thus, in Shakespearean tragedy, the protagonist's tragic experience is reflected, and often disparately manifested, in the other characters and their actions. Because the central light of the play expresses itself in various modes, implemented by its individual reception in different characters and instrumented through subsidiary actions, the audience experiences the drama as a cosmological event.

This is why Shakespearean drama provides a more comprehensive and realistic view of life than does Greek tragedy. Since the focus of classical tragedy strikes the protagonist only, the audience, enwrought solely by his suffering, totally identifies itself with him. The subordinate characters, therefore, simply react to his anguish or, at best, correspond with it. Shakespearean tragedy is a different matter. The minor characters do not merely react or correspond to the protagonist's calamity, but they respond individually and often quite differently to the dilemma that perplexes him. What destroys him often sustains them; what occasions his frustration frequently nurtures their life.

The effect, then, of Shakespearean tragedy is not wholly cathartic, for the emotional intensity of his plays is relaxed by incidental comic scenes, secondary plots, and other devices. Yet in all his tragedies predating *King Lear,* catharsis is perhaps the dominant effect, for the audience is primarily engrossed in the protagonist and his sufferings. Furthermore, because the protagonists in his earlier tragedies are *objectively* superior to the other characters, their tragic dignity, though imperiled by social forces and temporal considerations that would reduce their stature to that of common humanity, is sustained throughout the drama. Like the Greek heroes, they will not compromise themselves nor what they represent in order to concur with the demands of their society; they will not be comfortable. They will not traduce or demean their high office by deferring to the dictates which the milieu enforces upon lesser mortals.

But in *King Lear,* both protagonists lack this kind of heroic stature. Their pre-eminence is titular—not real; their offices dignify them. Lear is not "every inch a king" but instead accommodates his judgment to his daughters' flatteries and himself to the vicissitudes of time, his own subjectivity, and nature. He makes himself amenable to life's cajoleries by ineptly deferring to appearances, thus unconsciously effecting the disintegration of himself, his family, and the kingdom, so that he can "unburden'd crawl toward death." Though he retains the "name and all the addition to a king," he relinquishes the substance of that name by abnegating its responsibilities and authority. He becomes, therefore, king in appearance only.

The dramatic effect of *King Lear,* then, is one that transcends catharsis and befits a kind of drama that goes beyond tragedy. Because *King Lear* addresses the whole complexity of man's situation, not merely its tragic aspect, it cannot properly be construed as tragedy. That Shakespeare did not consider tragedy any longer adequate for expressing his views of the human condition should be apparent from his willfully flouting its conventions in *King Lear.* The view of life that *Lear* expresses is not tragic, but ironic. And the effect experienced by its audience is not catharsis, but what I would call *therapeusis.* My understanding of this term and its implications, as opposed to those of catharsis, will be elaborated in Chapter VII.

Enough has been said to support the contention that *King Lear* is not a tragedy in the orthodox sense; in many respects it is not even typical of Shakespearean tragedy. Clearly Shakespeare had dramatic intentions beyond the scope of tragedy or any other one dramatic genre. What then did he intend to accomplish by writing *King Lear*? The answer to this question will be supplied in the next chapter.

CHAPTER III

THE DRAMATIC COMPONENTS OF *KING LEAR*

More than a few eminent Shakespearean scholars have discredited *King Lear* as a tragedy and have asserted instead that Shakespeare was making use of conventions proper to other dramatic genres. Oscar James Campbell, for example, has maintained that *King Lear* is "a sublime morality play."[29]   K. W. Salter, in agreement that the morality element is strongly apparent in the play, notes parallels between a speech of Albany and a speech of God in *Everyman*.[30]   Thelma Nelson Greenfield also points out that the clothing motif in *King Lear* consistently complies with the medieval theological tradition.[31]   In an earlier observation, Tucker Brooke had commented upon the moral lessons derived from a study of the play,[32]   and Carolyn French subsequently has argued that King Lear presents a contrast of worldly wisdom and Christian folly,[33]   a contrast frequently treated in the medieval morality tradition. Campbell and others have noted that the characters of *King Lear* are modeled from the stock types found in the moralities and the Latin comedies.[34]

But in addition to sharing these characteristics found in the morality tradition, *King Lear's* affinities to the English chronicle plays of the sixteenth century are even more imposing. It is needless, perhaps, to point out that the title page of the first edition of *King Lear*, the "Pide Bull edition," or "Q_1", which appeared in 1608, read as follows: "M. William Shak-speare: *His True Chronicle Historie of the life and death of King Lear and his three Daughters. . . .* A later Quarto (Q_2), also bearing the date 1608, although recent investigation has determined that its actual date of issue was probably 1619, has almost the same title page as

---

[29]Oscar James Campbell, "The Salvation of Lear," *English Literary History*, XV (1948), 94.

[30]K. W. Salter, "Lear and the Morality Tradition," *Notes and Queries,* CXCIX (1954), 109f.

[31]Thelma Nelson Greenfield, "The Clothing Motif in *King Lear*," *Shakespeare Quarterly*, V (1954), 281-86.

[32]Tucker Brooke, "*King Lear* on the Stage," *Sewanee Review*, XXI (1913), 88-98.

[33]Carolyn S. French, "Shakespeare's 'Folly': *King Lear*," *Shakespeare Quarterly*, X (1959), 523-29.

[34]Campbell, *op. cit.,* 102.

Q_1.[35] These Quartos indicate clearly that the play definitely was composed, or at least considered, originally as a history play rather than a tragedy. It was not, in fact, designated a tragedy until it appeared as such in the 1623 First Folio edition, which, of course, appeared after Shakespeare's death. These facts certainly attest that *Lear* was intended as a chronicle play. The sources from which Shakespeare drew his material all purported to be historical accounts of the life and death of King Lear. Certainly the anonymous drama *King Leir,* with which undoubtedly Shakespeare was familiar and from which much of his incidental material derived, although he radically revised it, had borne the title "The True Chronicle History of King Leir and his three daughters Gonorill, Ragan, and Cordella." [36] It is, therefore, certainly not surprising that Irving Ribner includes *King Lear* , along with *Cymbeline,* among Shakespeare's history plays.[37]

Also prominently interspersed throughout the text of *Lear* are dramatic undertones suggesting the miracle and mystery play traditions that had flourished during the Middle Ages and had sporadically persisted even into Shakespeare's era. Most notable, perhaps, among the elements associated with medieval liturgical drama are the blending of paganistic and Christian traditions and the fusion of religious and secular interests in the play. Furthermore, the play abounds with ambiguities and anachronisms, two features characteristically common in the miracle plays of the fourteenth and fifteenth centuries. In addition, one might reasonably consider the virtuous characters in *Lear,* such as Cordelia, Edgar, and Albany, as corresponding to the sanctified personages that appear in the early English mystery plays. Especially the last scene of the play, with its allusions to the Last Judgment and Doomsday, establishes a connection to the miracle and morality traditions. George W. Williams has offered a considerable comment upon Shakespeare's allusions to the Deluge, the Last Judgment, and the "eschatological destruction" dealt with in the play.[38]

Theodore Spencer in his study of *King Lear* has come closer perhaps than any other scholar to envisioning the scope of the play. Though he does not consider the drama as an amalgam of most of the familiar dramatic types known to Shakespeare and his contemporaries,

[35]Steven Urkowitz, *Shakespeare's Revision of King Lear* (Princeton:Princeton University Press, 1980), p. 11.

[36]*Ibid.,* pp. 91-92.

[37]Irving Ribner, "Shakespeare and Legendary History: *Lear* and *Cymbeline,*" *Shakespeare Quarterly,* VII (1956), pp. 47-52.

[38]George W. Williams, "The Poetry of the Storm in *King Lear,*" *Shakespeare Quarterly,* II (1951), 67.

he is aware that the scope of the play exceeds that of any other Shakespearean drama.

> Shakespeare uses the three inter-related hierarchies given him by the assumptions of his age to make *King Lear* the largest and the most profound of all his plays. Nowhere else does he so completely fuse the contemporary concepts of the world, the individual and the state into a single unity; correspondences and parallels between them, amalgamations of one concept with another, are everywhere; they embody the vision of life and they form the texture of the style. . . .

> As we think of the techniques of this play, and it is with technique that we should begin, two words come at once to mind: re-inforcement and expansion. The sub-plot re-inforces the main plot; it is not, as in all the other plays where a sub-plot occurs, a contrast to it. Both Lear and Gloucester are the victims of filial ingratitude; the blinding of Gloucester is the physical equivalent to the madness of Lear; and both, as a result of their terrible experiences—though in very different degrees—achieve more wisdom at the end than they had at the beginning.[39]

Spencer's most important observation here is that Shakespeare in *Lear* achieves a fusion of "contemporary concepts of the world" nowhere so well integrated as in this play. The technique, he adds, by which this fusion is accomplished, involves re-inforcement and expansion. But, as Bradley had earlier pointed out, expansion, besides providing needed elaboration and re-inforcement, results in an

> . . .excess in the bulk of the material and the number of figures, events and movements, while they interfere with the clearness of vision. . . . They give the feeling of vastness, the feeling not of a scene or particular place, but of a world; or, to speak more accurately, of a particular place which is also a world.[40]

---

[39]Theodore Spencer, *Shakespeare and the Nature of Man,* Second Edition (New York: The Macmillan Company, 1949), pp. 135-36.

[40]Bradley, *op. cit.,* p. 261.

To complement the cosmological sense achieved through the dual plot, re-inforcement, and expansion, Shakespeare employs a number of dramatic genres, blended so as to imply the transcendence of Lear's universe to the realms of pure tragedy or comedy. The techniques cited by Spencer, though they lend credence to the macrocosmic world within which Lear and Gloucester live and function, supply only the external verities that spawn human experience. Corresponding to that macrocosm, the Lear universe, is the microcosmic world of Lear and Gloucester themselves, the *personal* world of the individual man. This microcosmic sense Shakespeare conveys primarily by incorporating into the play several dramatic vehicles instead of merely one. By blending diverse dramatic types, he not only portrays man from an emotional or tragic perspective, but also supplies to the human condition its complementary intellectual, moral, and historical aspects. The Lear universe, in fact, simulates the variety, the ambiguity, and the all-inclusiveness of life itself.

Since it has already been noted that many highly esteemed scholars have pertinently alluded to the several dramatic types represented in *King Lear*—e.g., the comedy, the chronicle, the morality, the mystery and miracle plays—it would be tedious and unnecessary to undertake a thorough exposition of all the genres developed in this drama. But perhaps a corroborative illustration of Shakespeare's use of the morality elements is needed to demonstrate his skillfully unobtrusive methodology. Chapter IV, therefore, will show how Shakespeare interpolates the morality tradition into the play without allowing that dimension to override the other equally important dramatic elements.

CHAPTER IV

THE MORAL CONTEXT OF *KING LEAR*

Among those who have addressed *King Lear* as a morality play, it is Professor Oscar J. Campbell who provides the most cogent and illuminating argument. In an article published in 1948, he points out the similarity of Lear to the typical central figure in the morality traditions. Summoned by death, Lear, like Everyman, tries to determine who his friends are, but following the fashion of the moralities, he errs in his appraisals of them.

> . . .Goneril and Regan, representing worldly goods and those insubstantial human relationships which are precariously cemented only by favors granted, grievously disappoint him. He suffers shattering disillusionment when he sees that their love has been an illusion, that they have been attached only to his power and possessions. The discovery that as soon as he strips himself of these, his ungrateful daughters scorn and reject him, reduces him to anger and despair. . . .

> Lear, then, is like mankind of both the Morality and homiletic tradition in that he has devoted his energies to the accumulation and worship of ephemeral possessions and to the pursuit of merely secular satisfactions.[41]

In addition, Campbell comments upon Lear's undertaking a Death-pilgrimage, as does the central character in most English morality plays of the fifteenth century.

> On his pilgrimage he is accompanied by two companions, and commentators, both of whom are creatures of Cynic-Stoic primitivism introduced into Elizabethan literature by way of Roman satire. These two are Kent, the stoic plain

---

[41]Campbell, *op. cit.*, 99.

man, and the Fool, or the wise innocent—each a child of Nature.[42]

Finally, Campbell asserts that the concluding action of the morality tradition, the purgation of the mankind representative, is also presented in *King Lear.* This purgation, he says, "comes when he awakens from the delusions of his frenzied mind to discover Cordelia and her unselfish, enduring love."[43]

Though plausible and illuminating, Campbell's argument would have been considerably strengthened had he observed that there are *seven* vicious characters in *King Lear* who correspond to the Seven Deadly Sins so often depicted in English morality plays.

Although these characters do not engage their virtuous counterparts in a formalized debate, as the Vices do in most medieval moralities, there are explicit rivalries between the vicious and the virtuous characters of the play. Admittedly, these combatants are not *merely* abstract personifications of the Virtues and Vices, as is invariably the case in most earlier moralities. Shakespeare's characters are too realistically drawn, too dramatically developed to represent only the several Virtues and Vices. But each *does* manifest a definite proclivity for a particular type of virtue or sin. My intent now is to show precisely which of the Seven Deadly Sins each of the vicious characters exemplifies and then to note in passing the virtuous character who is his rival.

The Duke of Burgundy, regarded as superfluous by many Shakespearean critics, appears but briefly in the first scene of the play and thereafter serves no dramatic purpose whatever. Nevertheless, Burgundy is essential to the play, for he represents the sin of Pride. In the opening scene, he is presented as a rival to France (Humility) for Cordelia's hand in marriage. A. C. Bradley, noting some of the improbabilities in *King Lear,* wonders why Burgundy rather than France should have first opportunity to marry Cordelia.[44] Apparently Burgundy is the preferred candidate simply because Cordelia, "new adopted" to Lear's hate, should, according to her father, be married to Pride. Lear believes that her noncompliance with his demand that she declare the extent of her love for him is motivated by pride, not honesty. Enraged, he exclaims, "Let pride, which she calls plainness, marry her." It is in deference to Burgundy's pride that Lear allows him priority to France.

---

[42]*Ibid.,* 102.

[43]*Ibid.,* 105-106.

[44]A. C. Bradley, *op. cit.,* 258.

The pride of Burgundy is best illustrated by his rejection of Cordelia. He spurns her because she has been stripped of her dowry and regal estate and is consequently no longer able to raise his fortunes or augment his renown and prestige. The destitute but virtuous Cordelia, undismayed, seems well contented that Burgundy has not accepted her:

> Peace be with Burgundy!
> Since that respect and fortune are his love,
> I shall not be his wife. (I, i, 250-52)

Burgundy is not satisfied with virtue itself unless a princely title and an attendant dowry go with it.

The sin of Wrath is represented by the "fiery Duke" of Cornwall, whose ultimate rival for Lear's kingdom is the patient Duke of Albany. Several references are made concerning Cornwall's irascible disposition. And as anger begets anger, so Cornwall often engenders anger in others. A good example of the conflagratory quality of wrath occurs in Act II, Scene ii, when Kent, already incensed, becomes infuriated by Cornwall's method of finding out the cause of Kent's antipathy to Oswald. Irate at Kent's audacity and blunt honesty, Cornwall reproves Kent for his conduct in the affair, but hardly examines Oswald. And since Kent's instinctive dislike for Oswald has voiced itself in rather plain terms, Cornwall rudely quiets Kent.

> Cornwall: Peace, sirrah!
> You beastly knave, know you no reverence?
> Kent: Yes, sir, but anger hath a privilege.
> (II, ii, 74-76)

Kent justifies his attacking Oswald by explaining that it was provoked by anger. Such provocation he knows that Cornwall, the representative of Wrath, would be likely to understand and perhaps excuse. But the plain-spoken Kent subsequently aggravates Cornwall's ire even more when he irreverently shows his disrespect for the whole company confronting him. For this offense, the incensed Cornwall has Kent put into the stocks, a punishment usually reserved for low criminals or petty thieves, certainly not a chastisement befitting the messenger of the king.

After Cornwall's departure, Gloucester visits Kent and commiserates with him and even offers to intercede for him:

> I am sorry for thee, friend. 'Tis the Duke's pleasure,
> Whose disposition, all the world well knows,
> Will not be rubb'd nor stopp'd. I'll entreat for thee.
> (II, ii, 158-161)

In the foregoing passage is the first direct reference to the Duke's disposition as one that "will not be rubb'd nor stopp'd"; *i. e.,* a disposition so vehement that it will not be mollified nor impeded.

In Act II, Scene iv, Lear, upset at finding Kent in the stocks, is further incensed when Gloucester reports that Cornwall and Regan refuse to speak to Lear. Again Gloucester remarks upon the incendiary temperament of Cornwall:

> My dear Lord,
> You know the fiery quality of the Duke,
> How unremovable and fix't he is
> In his own course. (II, iv, 92-95)

Lear, exceedingly wrought by Gloucester's observation, rejoins:

> My breath and blood!
> Fiery? The fiery Duke? Tell the hot Duke that—
> (II, ii, 104-105)

After this outburst and subsequent invectives, Lear demands that he be received. Finally, Regan and Cornwall appear, but only to treat him shabbily, coldly showing him only the slightest respect, while they warmly welcome Goneril, who arrives shortly thereafter. Then when the two sisters vie with each other in their efforts to humiliate the old king by reducing the number of his attendants, he leaves in a rage. A storm, which almost seems engendered by the tempestuous passions aroused in this scene, threatens outside the castle. Lear prefers the tempest outside to the one within.

Cornwall's "fiery quality" is next displayed after he is told of Gloucester's "treachery." He himself declares his anger when he sends servants to apprehend Gloucester:

> Though well we may not pass upon his life
> Without the form of justice, yet our power
> Shall do a court'sy to our wrath, which men
> May blame, but not control. (III, vii, 24-27)

Again Cornwall's rage is described, this time by himself, as being uncontrollable. Its cruelty vents itself later when he gouges out Gloucester's eyes, an act so merciless that a servant of Cornwall is enraged to rise against his lord and "take the chance of anger." The servant is slain by Regan from behind, but not before he deals Cornwall a fatal wound. So Cornwall expires, still in anger.

36

Although the villain Edmund may be "rough and lecherous," as his success with Goneril and Regan would indicate, still it is obvious that Edmund represents another vice that takes precedence over his lust. Early in the play his machinations and plots are employed against Edgar and Gloucester. In the famous "bastard" soliloquy, Edmund, the representative of Avarice, announces his intentions to deprive Edgar of his inheritance by wit:

> Well then,
> Legitimate Edgar, I must have your land.
> Our father's love is to the bastard Edmund
> As to th' legitimate. Fine word—' legitimate'!
> Well, my legitimate, if this letter speed,
> And my invention thrive, Edmund the base
> Shall top th' legitimate. I grow; I prosper.
> Now, gods, stand up for bastards! (I, ii, 14-22)

Edmund's mind and energies are bent toward supplanting his "generous" brother Edgar as heir to Gloucester's lands and revenue. And when this aim is accomplished, he is still unsatisfied. For Gloucester is yet alive, and the greedy Edmund wants his father's property not at some time in the uncertain future but in the present. Consequently, when the opportunity comes, Edmund, who has already betrayed and defrauded his brother, also betrays and supplants his father.

But even this is not sufficient to stanch the avarice of Edmund. Next he sees a possibility for further self-aggrandizement. By winning the affections of Goneril and/or Regan, he may rule Britain. He expresses no preference for either of Lear's "unnatural" daughters; either or both will do. He intends to wed the daughter that best serves his ambition.

> To both these sisters have I sworn my love;
> Each jealous of the other, as the stung
> Are of the adder. Which of them shall I take?
> Both? one? or neither? Neither can be enjoy'd
> If both remain alive. To take the widow
> Exasperates, makes mad her sister Goneril;
> And hardly shall I carry out my side,
> Her husband being alive. Now then, we'll use
> His countenance for the battle, which being done,
> Let her who would be rid of him devise
> His speedy taking off. (V, i, 55-65)

His great personal magnetism (which incidentally suggests an acquisitive nature that draws other people and their possessions to him) serves his cupidity. All causes, passions, natural graces, and charms—his filial obligations, his "loves," and his honor—are sacrificed to his all-consuming avarice.

Lear's eldest daughter, Goneril, from her initial speech, in which she expresses an immoderate "love" for her father, to her expiration in the name of her "love" for Edmund in Act V, is governed by her lust. Her proclamation of excessive love for her father in the first scene rivals the chaste declaration of Cordelia, who loves "according to her bond." If a vice can be measured by the sacrifices one makes to it, then lust—to which Goneril sacrifices honor, estate, father, husband, sisters, and finally her own life—clearly is her consuming passion. Her very name offers a valuable clue to her lustful nature. The spelling and the sound of "Goneril" suggest an unpleasant venereal disease, "gonorrhea," which is often the result of inordinate sexual activity.

Before Goneril, who, with the possible exception of Edmund, is the most aggressive character in the play, initiates the malevolent, ungrateful mistreatment of Lear, she tells Regan that something must be done, "and in the heat." "In the heat" aptly describes the characteristic temper of the aggressive, "bitchy" Goneril. Furthemore, she is peculiarly sensitive to lustful behavior in others, finding and even projecting lust where it probably does not exist. The irony of her statement concerning the behavior of Lear's knights is almost blatant:

> Here do you keep a hundred knights and squires;
> Men so disorder'd, so debosh'd and bold
> That this our court, infected with their manners,
> Shows like a riotous inn. Epicurism and lust
> Make it more like a tavern or a brothel
> Than a grac'd palace. (I, iv, 262-67)

After this rebuke, Lear leaves Goneril's castle invoking a curse which imports the character of Goneril. He calls down sterility upon her; her lust is to be non-productive, barren.

> Hear, Nature, hear! dear goddess, hear!
> Suspend thy purpose, if thou didst intend
> To make this creature fruitful.
> Into her womb convey sterility;
> Dry up in her the organs of increase;
> And from her derogate body never spring
> A babe to honor her! If she must teem,
> Create her child of spleen, that it may live
> And be a thwart disnatur'd torment to her.
> (I, iv, 297-305)

38

Her lust, the unnatural perversion of love, if it bring forth at all, should produce unnatural, or perverse, offspring.

Act IV, Scene ii portrays Goneril's return to her palace accompanied by Edmund. After describing her husband as a milquetoast and indicating thereby that she has no relish of his virtue, Goneril gives Edmund a favor and declares her love. Her loathing of Albany recalls a ghost's assessment of lust in another Shakespearean play:

> But virtue, as it never will be mov'd,
> Though lewdness court it in a shape of heaven,
> So lust, though to a radiant angel link'd,
> Will sate itself in a celestial bed,
> And prey on garbage. (*Hamlet,* I, v, 52-56)

Accordingly, Goneril prefers Edmund's magnetic, animalistic charm to Albany's patient, compassionate love:

> My most dear Gloucester!
> O, the difference of man and man!
> To thee a woman's services are due;
> My fool usurps my body. (IV, ii, 25-28)

Attending upon Goneril and abetting her lust is the eunuch-like steward Oswald, who, when he is slain by Edgar, bears on his person a letter from Goneril to Edmund. Edgar, upon reading the letter, is disgusted with the "murtherous lechers" and appalled at the "indistinguished space of woman's will." The word "will" is common in Elizabethan parlance for "desire" in the sense of "lust." (*Cf. Hamlet,* III, iv, 88)

Goneril's sister Regan represents the sin of Envy. Like Goneril, she is Cordelia's rival for Lear's affection. Throughout the play, in contrast to Cordelia's charity, Regan's envy endeavors to usurp or surpass the accomplishments of others. In her first speech, she emulates Goneril's profession of love for Lear, *only* she claims that Goneril's love "comes too short."

> Sir, I am made
> Of the selfsame metal that my sister is,
> And prize me at her worth. In my true heart
> I find she names my very deed of love;
> Only she comes too short, that I profess
> Myself an enemy to all other joys
> Which the most precious square of sense possesses,
> And find that I am alone felicitate
> In your dear Highness' love. (I, i, 70-78)

Characteristically, Regan is not content merely to *equal* Goneril in love; her profession of love must *go beyond* Goneril's.

Furthermore, at a later point in the play, after Goneril has "disquantitied" Lear's train, Regan feels that she must outdo her sister's cruelty to their father. Informed that Goneril has abused Lear, Regan determines to be even more cruel. At first, she refuses to speak to him, thereby showing him greater disrespect than Goneril had done. Then when Goneril arrives at Gloucester's castle, the two daughters vie with each other in torturing the old man. When Goneril insists that Lear reduce his retinue to twenty-five, then ten, then five, Regan suggests that he needs no retinue at all.

> Goneril: Hear me, my Lord.
> What need you five-and -twenty, ten or five,
> To follow in a house where twice so many
> Have a command to tend you?
> Regan: What need one? (II, iv, 263-67)

Regan, though she seldom initiates evil, almost invariably attempts to intensify or pre-empt the villainy begun by another. Thus, when Cornwall harshly puts Kent into the stocks, exclaiming:

> Fetch forth the stocks! As I have life and honor,
> There shall he sit till noon. (II, ii, 140-41),

Regan extends his cruelty by prolonging Kent's tenure:

> Till noon? Till night, my lord, and all night too.
> (II, ii, 142)

Again, when Cornwall resolves to gouge out one of Gloucester's eyes, Regan exceeds his initiate cruelty by adding:

> One side will mock another. Th' other too.
> (III, vii, 71)

Because Goneril first lusts for Edmund's love, Regan invidiously wants him too. He is especially desirable to Regan now that Goneril heatedly pursues him. She is once again seeking to appropriate what another claims. She even vies with Goneril for Oswald's service, finally succeeding in enlisting him *also* to deliver *her* letter to Edmund. Vying with her sister, she hints in her note that she is a more "convenient" candidate for Edmund's favor than Goneril is:

> Therefore I do advise you to take this note.

My lord is dead; Edmund and I have talk'd,
And more convenient is he for my hand
Than for your lady's. . . . (IV, v, 29-32)

In her competition with Goneril, Regan employs Edmund to lead her
forces against the French, thereby attempting to appropriate Edmund for
herself. She asserts that it is she rather than Goneril who can best raise
Edmund's worldly estate.

Throughout the play, Regan's invidious nature adds fuel to whatever
fire is raging. She extends Gloucester's suffering (II, i) by suggesting
that the knights attending upon Lear have probably contributed to the
delinquency of the banished Edgar. It is she who demands that the
doors of Gloucester's palace be shut to Lear, as she enlarges again
upon the dangers that might be incurred by admitting "Lear's desperate
train." (II, iv, 307-310) It is typical of the invidious mind to conjure up
such non-existent evils in order to justify its own malice. It is Regan, not
satisfied with merely baiting Gloucester, who plucks the old man by the
beard, an act showing disrespect and irreverence to old age and to her
host. Such intolerance and ingratitude are concomitants of envy, which
refuses to pay homage or respect to anything not its own nor serving its
purposes.

It is not at once apparent which of the Seven Deadly Sins Oswald
represents. Like most of the vicious characters in the play, he manifests
his villainy in sundry ways. Already it has been pointed out that he
serves Goneril by acting as intermediary between her and Edmund; and
since Goneril represents Lust, one would justifiably infer his function as
a pander to her lascivious appetites. Note that he does service only for
her; he does not serve Albany. His attendance upon a libidinous
mistress would perhaps suggest that he is eunuch-like, since he is privy
to all her undertakings and since he apparently enjoys and willingly
promotes the ends she seeks.

The play also places emphasis upon his unmanly behavior with its
portrayal of his cowardly reaction to Kent's assaults upon him in Act I,
Scene ii. His fearful flight from combat with Kent in this scene, as well as
the epithets that Kent hurls at him, gives credence to his unmanliness.
Kent identifies him as

> A knave; a rascal; an eater of broken meats; a
> base, proud, shallow, beggarly, three-suited,
> hundred-pound, filthy, worsted-stocking knave; a
> lily-liver'd, action-taking, whoreson, glass-gazing,
> superserviceable, finical rogue; one-trunk-
> inheriting slave; one that wouldst be a bawd in way
> of good service, and art nothing but the

composition of a knave, beggar, coward, pandar,
and the son and heir of a mongrel bitch; one whom
I will beat into clamourous whining, if thou deny the
least syllable of thy addition.   (II, ii, 15-25)

His servility is suggested by "three-suited," "super-serviceable," "bawd,"
"beggar," and "pandar"; his cowardice by "lily-liver'd," "action-taking,"
"coward," and "clamourous whining"; and his effeminacy by "shallow,"
"worsted-stocking," "whoreson," "glass-gazing," "finical," and "the son
and heir of a mongrel bitch."

But in addition to having an obviously unmanly spirit, he seems also
to be quite flabby physically. A close scrutiny of the play as it alludes to
Oswald will bear out that he is uncommonly fat, and since corpulence is
usually the result of excessive eating, it seems plausible to contend that
Oswald represents the sin of Gluttony.

Note, first of all, that Oswald is Goneril's *steward.* A steward is a
person in charge of a large household or estate, one whose duties
include supervision of the kitchen and household servants; *i. e.,* one
whose duties are domestic. Etymologically the word *steward* derives
from the Middle English compound, *stiward,* or one who is the keeper of
a sty; and a sty pretty well describes the domicile of a Goneril, or for that
matter, the residence of a "pig" like Oswald. So, in a sense, we may
think of Oswald as the keeper of a sty, in which he also feeds and
maintains himself.

It is noteworthy too that Oswald, when he makes his first appearance
in the play (I, iii), is dismissed by Goneril with the command to "prepare
for dinner," a command which indicates his concern with food. This
seems unimportant, even trivial, but if one observes the terms used in
Goneril's conversation with Oswald in this scene, he will perhaps be
surprised at the frequency of words and phrases pertaining to the
gustatory sense, to obesity, and to general flaccidity. Goneril tells
Oswald that Lear every hour "flashes into one *gross* crime or other," that
if he (Oswald) "come *slack* of former services," he will "do well." She
advises him to put on "*weary negligence,*" and if the "idle old man," Lear,
"*distaste* it," he can visit Regan. She does not care "what *grows* of it."

But it is chiefly in his encounters with Kent that the impression of
Oswald's obesity is best enforced. Kent's references to Oswald
repeatedly suggest the latter's corpulence. When he "trips up Oswald's
heels (I, iv), Kent defies the cowardly steward to "measure your lubber's
length again," but Oswald flees. In Act II, Scene ii, the two meet again.
Once more Kent aggressively affronts Oswald, besieging him with
epithets that no honorable man with heart would tolerate. He refers to

Oswald as "an eater of broken meats"; *i. e.*, one who, after others have sufficiently dined, gluttonously devours the remaining victuals. Challenging Oswald to draw his sword, Kent declares that he will "make a sop of the moonshine o' you." The image is appropriate, since Oswald's appetite is no doubt such that he is wont "to sop up" the gravies and other rich sauces when he is dining. Furthermore, he threatens to "carbonado" Oswald's shanks. "Carbonado" is a term in cookery which means "to slash a piece of meat for broiling." Kent therefore is implying that Oswald is a piece of meat, whose fleshy shanks offer an inviting target to Kent's blade. When this quarrel is interrupted, Oswald significantly declares that he is "scarce in breath," a phrase again suggesting corpulence; his shortwindedness implies his physical condition. Later, Kent explains to Cornwall his reason for inciting the quarrel and refers to Oswald as a "goose," a fowl whose plump physique requires no further comment. Then he puns upon the word "fleshment" in describing Oswald's previous slighting of Lear.

The next reference to Oswald occurs when Lear discovers his messenger in the stocks. Inquiring the cause of Kent's predicament, Lear receives the following report:

> My lord, when at their home
> I did commend your Highness' letters to them,
> Ere I was risen from the place that show'd
> My duty kneeling, came there a reeking post,
> Stew'd in his haste, half breathless, panting forth
> From Goneril his mistress salutations; . . .
> (II, iv, 27-32)

Oswald is described as being "half breathless," another reference to his shortness of wind. Further, Oswald arrived "a reeking post, stew'd in his haste." In other words, like the meat in a stew, the fleshy *steward* was perspiring heavily.

Gluttony, therefore, appears to be Oswald's primary vice, and it, an appetite of the body, is properly allied to Lust. The abstemious Kent, who throughout the play deplores excess and urges moderation, as Oswald's antithesis, cannot endure the self-indulgent steward.

Curan belatedly appears in one scene only and indeed seems quite unnecessary, for he contributes little, if anything, by way of dramatic action. He informs Edmund (II, i) that Cornwall is to visit Gloucester's castle and that there are rumors of a civil war brewing. Yet he elaborates not all but states this news lackadaisically, leaving its details and pertinence for Edmund to piece out and use as best he can. His niggardly speech, his tardy habit, and his brief sojourn on the stage indicate that he is meant to represent Sloth. He is too indolent to expatiate upon the momentous news he bears; yet his listless curiosity and his bent for spreading rumors and hearkening to the latest gossip typify the avocations most pleasant to idle minds.

The introduction of Curan, unless he appears in order to complete the parade of the Seven Deadly Sins, seems superfluous. Except to depict Sloth, there is no reason for Shakespeare's presenting a new character. A messenger, a lord, or any *nameless* attendant could have supplied Edmund with this information.

His brief and tardy appearance, his paucity of speech, his apathy at an impending event of great import—all testify a nature lethargic and difficult to arouse. After briefly informing Edmund of the prospects for war, he withdraws, apparently unconcerned and too lazy to take any further part in the play.

Each vicious character with the exception of Curan, whose virtuous corollary is the Fool (Industry), directly engages his adversary in antagonistic rivalry. But Curan, true to his slothful nature, does not possess sufficient energy to confront the Fool, who, in contrast, is so diligent in his service to Lear that he has no time for extraneous activities.

Admittedly, these seven vicious characters give only a rough impersonation of the Seven Deadly Sins. They are not mere sinful abstractions parading across the stage; they are dramatically plausible human beings. And by imbuing them with dramatic veracity, Shakespeare has vivified the old morality tradition and fulfilled its potentialities by making it smack of human life. Abstract moralism frequently deadens rather than enlivens the human conscience, but a graphic illustration, such as *King Lear* affords, of man's moral involvement in the affairs of life makes the deadly effects of sin meaningful and real. While it is true that all of *Lear's* vicious characters partake of several types of sin, it is equally true that each of them is primarily motivated by one dominant vice. All the Deadly Sins are interrelated; all savor of the others; yet they are also cognizable as distinct and particular taints that undermine and destroy character and the human soul. Shakespeare has demonstrated in *King Lear* that any one of the Deadly Sins involves its actor in other sins as well. He has clearly shown that sinful exercises inevitably lead to death.

The foregoing analysis of the moral context of the play indicates that *King Lear,* if it is a tragedy, is also much more. Though I have restricted my observations in this chapter to the morality elements so amply represented throughout the play, it is no less true that features of the chronicle, tragic, and comic traditions are just as abundantly presented, and so finely enwrought are they into the fabric of *Lear* that none obtrusively overrides the other dramatic elements. So well knit, in fact, are these dramatic strands that only with keen discernment can one distinguish them. Yet the effect achieved by *King Lear* is not simply a composite result of Shakespeare's blending these dramatic genres. The dominant effect produced by the play, at least upon a mind unbiased by dramatic preconceptions, is ironic rather than tragic. Perhaps the tragic response is precluded in part by the presentation of "views or attitudes. . diametrically opposed in such a way that each must logically exclude the others."[45]   But such an explanation does not wholly account for the play's failure to accomplish a tragic response, though admittedly it is difficult for a protagonist to elicit an unambiguous emotional reaction when he assumes no consistent "heroic" stance, when his society and his personal status are so unstable that he is yo-yoed from the zenith of life to its nadir, from king to naked beggar, from opulence to penury, from absolute authority to utter dependency. The very complexity of the play, together with its non-commital outlook that yields freedom from a partisan view of the human dilemma, prohibits a purely tragic response. It appears, in fact, that Shakespeare with *King Lear* has developed a new dramatic mode, far more comprehensive and undeluded than what is afforded by any previous play.

While Shakespeare and his dramatic predecessors had in earlier works made use of irony, they had done so in order to achieve either a tragic or comic effect. It would seem, however, that in *King Lear* Shakespeare reversed the procedure and used tragedy and comedy to produce an ironic effect. In the next chapter an inquiry concerning the nature of irony will be undertaken, and the ironic effect produced by the play will be considered in detail.

---

[45]McElroy, *Shakespeare's Mature Tragedies*, p. 161.

CHAPTER V

THE SUBSTANCE OF THE IRONIC DRAMA

Concerning irony, far too many scholars have narrowed its implications. They have seldom noted that the ironic sense proceeds not merely from an awareness of discrepancy between what seems to be and what is, but that this perception depends upon a much ampler awareness than that required for the perception of paradox. For irony transcends, even as it pervades, the partisanship which characterizes the perspectives, or philosophical stances, from which life is usually interpreted. What seems needed, then, is *clarification:* not so much another definition of irony as an expatiation of the inadequate definitions already current. My intention, therefore, is to present, not a definition of irony, but an appreciation and appraisal of the ironic conception of life as depicted in *King Lear.*

Essentially, irony results from the perception of incongruities between appearance and reality: it depends upon a realization that discrepancies exist between what seems, or is acknowledged, to be true and what is really true. Those appearances to which convention gives the staunchest credibility are designated as *facts.* Facts are normally held in such esteem that one seldom questions their veracity; they are generally regarded as not only true themselves but as the best certified touchstones for ascertaining other truths.

But facts are credited as truthful only because they are sustained and corroborated by certain faculties of apprehension resident in the human being. These faculties—the senses, the intellect, the emotions, and the will—are the vehicles through which fact makes itself known. But since these faculties are not equally developed in all persons and because factors—such as convention, environment, heredity, past experiences—affect its complexion, fact is ambiguously understood. And when one recognizes that fact is ambiguous and that "it speaks a various language," one experiences irony. A thrilling shock of awareness results from the disclosure that fact is merely a credible shell importing multiple meanings validated only by the testimony of the several human faculties variously developed.

This ironic shock, which brings a measure of illumination and truth to the formerly illuded individual, accomplishes a kind of *stasis,* whereby he enjoys a "sabbatical leave" from the vicissitudes of life that previously deluded him. The *stasis* succeeding the ironic shock resolves the conflict between appearance and reality by recognizing their commutuality and thereby liberating the individual from the victimization

47

of what he formerly thought was fact or truth. The fact, however, which he had categorically considered truth, we must remember, has been ratified by the *separate* testimony of his senses, his emotions, his will, or his reason, or perhaps by the dictates of social convention—not by realization grounded in a *conjunctive* experience embracing all these various cognitive modes. Hence, the facts that he had subscribed to, that he had believed indubitably true, were based solely upon the peculiar stance from which he addressed them. What he had confidently designated as the truth, solidly based upon some single substantive resource of his own self or upon his social experience, was in reality only a partial truth—an obsession or, at best, an illusion perpetrated by his own psychic one-sidedness.

But before some of the outstanding features of irony can be profitably discussed and applied to *King Lear* and ironic drama, it is needful to consider a few prevailing conceptions about irony.

One aspect of irony sharply emphasized by Robert Boies Sharpe is its relationship to impersonation. Since irony depends upon the manifestation of reality through appearances and since the very basis of drama is impersonation, drama is essentially ironic. When a play commences, the spectator, knowing that the actor is posing as what he is not, is therefore fully aware that contradictions between reality and appearance exist.[46] But it is through the falsehood, or impersonation, which pervades drama, that reality is manifested:

> In the minds of playwright, director, actor, and
> audience (all must co-operate to make a play), the
> drama is perceived by the senses and felt in the
> emotions as *art,* that is, as reality or "nature"
> heightened for beauty by human means. This is a
> mixed, complicated, even somewhat sophisticated
> state or mood. It is a mood we call *ironic,* because
> of its simultaneous perception of the two concepts
> *art* and *nature* as at the same time contradictory
> and harmonious, untrue and true. In the ironic
> mood one is conscious of contradictions but is
> above being frustrated by them; rather, one
> includes them in a single perception. . .[47]

Sharpe considers the ironic mood as a percipient state not at all troubled by the contradictions generated by the attempts of dramatic art

---

[46]Robert Boies Sharpe, *Irony in the Drama* (Chapel Hill: The University of North Carolina Press, 1959), p. vii.
[47]*Ibid.,* p. viii.

to impersonate reality, or "nature." He does not, however, stress the fact that drama is an artistic "language," which effectively conveys the truth only when its conventions, or "terminology," are properly employed by playwright and actors and rightly understood by the audience. Frustrations and misunderstandings result when any one of the dramatic principals (playwright, director, actors, and audience) cannot decipher the language (art) of the play or translate it into the truth of "nature." The ironic perception is the decoder and the translator needed to reconcile the opposition existing between artistic appearance and the reality of nature. Without ironic awareness, the contradictions between appearance and reality breed discord and perplexity.

Sharpe goes on to point out that theatrical irony in the act of impersonation correlates to verbal irony, since neither intends to defraud or deceive but to "be seen through." The purpose of both is to reveal, not conceal, the truth.

> The actor's form of impersonation (not a swindling on the street but a playing on the stage) is inherently ironic, as we see by its paralleling the verbal or "straight" form of irony we often call sarcasm. Ironic praise is not meant to deceive or to flatter, but to be seen through and to gain its abrasive effect by the artistic contradiction of word by meaning; similarly, the actor does not wish us to believe that he *is* Hamlet, but to admire his artistic imitation of Hamlet. The sarcastic man's irony is not a lie; the actor's impersonation is not a fraud.[48]

Essentially, Sharpe here points out that the ironic purpose is the revelation of truth through statements, actions, or situations which seem to contradict or belie reality. Interestingly enough, irony would appear to be the opposite of hypocrisy, for hypocrisy intends through its impersonation to deceive. The hypocrite represents himself as being better than he is by playing a role which he would have one to believe is not a role; the ironist, on the other hand, intends no deception but hopes to manifest truth through his impersonation. The hypocrite either consciously or unconsciously admits his inferiority to his role by preferring to represent himself as being otherwise than what he is. Conversely, the ironist expresses reality by understatement and self-diminution. The role he plays is not adopted for self-aggrandizement but for the sake of the truth he wishes to express. His own person is kept under cover. Whereas the hypocrite overstates his pretense, the ironist understates reality. G. G. Sedgewick observes that understatement, or

---

[48] *Ibid.,* ix.

litotes, has "an abundant, if somewhat cloistered, life" and that litotes was the ironic method most often employed by Socrates.[49] Sedgewick, in fact, intimates that not only the impact of Socrates upon his contemporaries, but the dramatic effect of irony itself, may be largely the results of understating reality.

But the ironic posture to which I have been pointing alludes not simply to an awareness of the clash of word with meaning, or appearance with reality, nor to the litotic inadequacy of mere statement to communicate the fullness of truth, but to the mental habit , or rather the spiritual disposition, that beholds such conflicts. The ironist views the incongruities and contradictions unfolding before him, yet is undeluded by them; instead, he sees their interconnectedness, and if he happens to be creative, he gives them form and order.

The spectator's enjoyment during a play's performance may well be the result of his detachment from the spectacle and the dramatic entanglement in which the performers are involved. Because he comprehends the drama as a whole and knows the significance of the actors' statements and actions, he experiences delight as the drama unfolds. He is pleased because he transcends the viewpoints and the limited perceptions of the dramatic characters, all of whom are painfully or absurdly unaware of the full import of their statements and actions. While they are enmeshed in the dramatic net and, therefore, imperfectly aware of the signification of what they do and say, he enjoys a god-like perspective: he sees all and knows all that is going on. The drama gratifies his quest for meaning, for he understands the significance of the characters' behavior, while they are only semi-conscious of what they say and do.

With similar satisfaction, the ironist observes the realities of life in much the same way that the spectator regards drama. He surveys the activities of life and sees their interconnections, relations, and purposes; and since he is aware of reality and because he accepts it, he is the antithesis of the hypocrite, who is unaware of reality or afraid to acknowledge it.

Because his perspective withholds *commitment* to the issues posed by the situations of life, the ironist primarily concerns himself with meanings or significances expressed through the sundry activities of life, whereas the partisan observer or participant is mostly concerned with the activities themselves; or rather, to express the idea more succinctly, the ironist pays attention to the "how" or "why" while other people regard

---

[49]G. G. Sedgewick, *Of Irony: Especially in the Drama* (Toronto: The University of Toronto Press, 1948), pp. 6-7.

the "what." That Shakespeare was a supreme ironist partly accounts for the incongruities and inconsistencies that abound in *King Lear.* A. C. Bradley, after pointing out several of these incongruities, attempts a somewhat inadequate justification of them.[50]

Confessing his bewilderment at Shakespeare's apparent carelessness in regard to consistency, definiteness, and dramatic congruity in this drama, Bradley rationalizes Shakespeare's recurrent negligence by admitting a possible purpose for it. Shakespeare's carelessness, according to Bradley, results in a "vagueness" that gives us a feeling "of vastness"; Shakespeare has shunned particularities, "proper names," in order to provide the sense of a cosmos. By interfering with our "clearness of vision," so Bradley reasons, these incongruous, vague elements tend to make a more effective appeal to our imaginations.

Perhaps so. But if, as I contend, Shakespeare's intention in *Lear* is to convey the ironic perspective, then the "vagueness" of the play simply reflects a candid unconcern with the phenomenal world; the focus of the ironic playwright quite naturally dwells upon the subjective reality of the *Lear* universe, not upon the objective circumstances that ambiguously express it. (In fact, the "obscurities," "shadowy forests," "indefiniteness," and improbabilities all suggest the ambiguity of phenomena, the relativity of all concreteness.) The externalized Lear himself (his embodiment), when he is regarded objectively as a phenomenon, is only vaguely the real Lear; or, as the Fool admirably expresses it, he is "Lear's shadow."

King Lear, a drama that seems almost contemptuous of the phenomenon, concentrates one's interest upon the psychological dynamics of the characters. Where Cornwall lives, why Burgundy gets first chance at Cordelia, why Edmund forges a letter rather than fabricate a conversation—all such questions are impertinences to the ironist; they elicit at best merely intellectual curiosity. "What" happens and "when" and "where" it occurs are incidental to the main focus of *King Lear;* the phenomenology of the play often seems gratuitous and purely accidental, and it stirs the interest only of journalists and gossips. Through the employment of anachronisms, secular inconsistencies, incongruous actions, and vagueness of localities, the play testifies that reality is free to express itself in any terms available, even in contradictory terms. Furthermore, it shows that any person absorbed in the "what" is subject to all sorts of confusion and ambiguities. But if one sees through the "what," his interest is transferred to its underlying reality. W. H. Clemen rightly understands Shakespeare's concentration

---

[50]A. C. Bradley, *op. cit.,* pp. 257-260.

upon the internal psychology and his neglect of external affairs as constituting the primary interest of *King Lear.*

> The middle acts of the tragedy, Acts II-IV, are the richest in imagery. The outer action is less important here and is relegated to the background. The main emphasis does not fall upon the outer course of events, upon what Regan or Goneril is planning, or what Edmund is about, but rather upon what is passing in Lear himself. The outer drama has become an inner drama. Beneath the surface of the plot lies the deeper level of inner experience which gradually frees itself more and more from the sparse events of the action. The latter becomes a frame and an occasion in order that the former may take on living reality. In truth, Shakespeare has not treated this outer action with the same thoroughness and care as he usually employed in the construction of the plot. As Bradley has already pointed out, the plot displays a number of inconsistencies and is not carried out clearly. Goethe found the action of Lear full of improbabilities, and "absurd." But Shakespeare was concerned not with the "outer," but with the "inner " drama ....[51]

Clemen agrees with Bradley that the world of *King Lear* is a cosmos in its own right. But the *Lear* cosmos is not clearly definable by the coventional way in which one regards and interprets the universe; not all events in Shakespeare's play are causally concatenated or sequentially consistent, as one is accustomed to think that the historical process must be.[52] But significantly enough, the historical Lear and Shakespeare's Lear bear only slight resemblance to each other. For Shakespeare seems unconcerned with historical details; he is not especially interested in "what" the historical Lear supposedly did so much as in "why" he did it. Nor does it even significantly matter "what" Lear does in the play. Another person might perform the same actions that Lear performs, yet be totally different from Lear. The action, or the

---

[51]W. H. Clemen, *The Development of Shakespeare's Imagery* (Cambridge, Mass.: Harvard University Press, 1951), p. 136.

[52]Again see Mack's *King Lear in Our Time,* pp. 77-80. Like Bradley and Clemen, he points out some of 'the fluidities and contradictions' of the play, but his conclusion is that *Lear* addresses us in much the same way as do our dreams by presenting a world in which 'people and events possess circumstantial reality for each of us, yet at the same time. . .function. . .as huge cloudy symbols of a history generic to all human beings, . . .'

"what," is ambiguous. Realizing this, Shakespeare consequently was interested with establishing not the "what," but its validity or reality. What Lear does and says *could* be done and said by others under the same or different circumstances. The important thing is not what he does but who he is. Lear's subjective status is more significant that his external actions or his objective appearance. Shakespeare authenticates Lear's acts by providing the underlying subjective reality that engenders them.

An act which lacks this subjective reality, though its repercussions might be spectacular and even fraught with considerable mundane consequence, is spiritually meaningless—an empty gesture. The ironist often sees in the phenomenal world an act that he fails to note, for he senses the unreality of its actor; but the ironist regards as meaningful the same act if it is performed by some other person possessing subjective reality. It is the reality expressing itself through the phenomenon that engages the attention of the ironist; the ordinary person, on the other hand, is concerned with the phenomenon and its actuality.

Since the ironist attunes himself to the reality underlying appearance, he will be unmoved by circumstances or by happenings as such, for actuality scarcely concerns him. His ironical outlook stoically accepts the truth, regardless of the relative or manifest aspects projected by reality into the phenomenal world. The ironist is not involved in "interesting" events, because his interest is not in what happens; events are, to him, merely outward manifestations of a reality which may paradoxically express itself. Neither is he an enthusiast, for he is not the victim of a partisan view of life. When he assumes a point of view, he does so facetiously for the sake of communication, always aware that the adopted viewpoint is inadequate and partial; in truth, he is neither "for" nor "against" the phenomenon. The phenomenon simply manifests; it is not, in itself, reality.

Knowing that it is subjective reality or *spirit* which enkindles and sustains existence, the ironist nonetheless is also aware that the sense of security and certitude upon which the mass of men depends is not founded upon spirit but is based upon the apparentness of the phenomenon. Intact in this knowledge, the ironist cannot yield to the whims of circumstance, nor can he be enslaved by the conventions prevalent during the era of his existence. As an ironist, he finds all convention dubious, for he realizes the ambiguous, paradoxical nature of existence. His ironic discernment enables him at once to detect from the spoken or written word whether it is a tried and experienced man who speaks.

As he matured, Shakespeare, with supreme ironic insight, realized the limitations of tragedy and comedy and saw that both presented only partisan views of life. Up to then, like his dramatic predecessors, he had used irony in the service of tragedy and comedy; but he perceived that in reality, in life itself, tragedy and comedy served irony. Realizing that the truth of life lay in neither tragedy nor comedy but beyond both, he arrived at the ironic conception of life described by Friedrich Nietzsche:

> I no longer feel in common with you; the very cloud which I see beneath me, the blackness and heaviness at which I laugh—that is your thundercloud.
> Ye look aloft when ye long for exaltation; and I look downward because I am exalted.
> Who among you can at the same time laugh and be exalted?
> He who climbeth on the highest mountains laugheth at all tragic plays and tragic realities.[53]

Therefore, in his later maturity, Shakespeare abandoned his writing of tragedies, the dramatic efficacy of which he realized had lain in irony. (Reversal of situation and recognition are simply two different expressions of irony. Reversal of situation implies that one point of view has been exchanged for another; recognition implies that one sees something in a new light, that one has penetrated the appearance and discerned the reality.) Shakespeare, realizing that tragedy and comedy are simply ways of viewing life incompletely or prejudicially, forsook both as ends, employed them as means, and produced his great ironical drama, *King Lear.*

---

[53]Friedrich Nietzsche, "Thus Spake Zarathustra," tr. Thomas Common, *The Philosophy of Nietzsche* (New York: Random House, Inc., 1954), p. 40.

CHAPTER VI

IRONY IN *KING LEAR*

Irony is not merely the predominant rhetorical device used in *King Lear* but also the primary source of interest in the play. In the drama there is scarcely an action, a statement, or a feeling expressed that is not ironic. From the commencement to the end of the play, irony is implicitly, if not overtly, present in almost every utterance and action. The first line in the play, spoken by Kent:

> I thought the King had more affected the Duke of Albany
> than Cornwall. (I, i, 1-2)

suggests the tentativeness of judgments based on appearances, while at the same time it shows, ironically, that Lear's instinct regarding Albany and Cornwall is accurate even if his judgment is faulty. One of the key motifs of the drama is hereby unobtrusively announced: the befuddled state of knowledge which arises from observing merely the appearances of things. Subsequent actions of the play will graphically illustrate the disastrous effects that follow when decisions and judgments are based upon such tentative opinions as this. It is here in the first scene that one is forewarned about the incertitude occasioned by judging from appearances. Ironically, Edmund seems quite attractive in this scene, despite his illegitimacy, if one is to judge by appearances only. He is polite and deferential to his elders. But, as we will discover when we get to know him, his seemingly virtuous behavior disguises the arch-villain of the play.

Though its setting is pagan, *King Lear* exemplifies most pronouncedly the Christian idea that the passing of judgment is fraught with serious consequences, not merely to the judged but to the judge (*New Testament,* "Matthew," 7:1-2). This idea is cogently enforced by the crucial incidents of the play. Both Lear and Gloucester are persons of authority whose demises are wrought by the consequences of their passing judgments upon other people. Lear brings tragedy upon himself when he arbitrarily banishes Kent and disinherits Cordelia for telling him the truth. To his deluded mind their virtues *appear* to be vices. And consistent with Aristotle's dictum that the tragic protagonist's *harmartia* (variously construed as a "moral flaw," "an error in judgment," or "a misstep") rather than willful wickedness procures catastrophe, Gloucester's tragedy, like Lear's, derives from false judgment. He misjudges Edgar guilty of treason and intended parricide, and his ruin follows this error in judgment.

It is perhaps banal to point out that Lear's and Gloucester's sufferings, both the results of erroneous judgment, are alleviated only when those faculties by which they had misapprehended the truth are destroyed: Lear begins to understand reality after he loses his reason; Gloucester, when he loses his sight. Misapprehension caused by faulty reasoning has led to Lear's decline; misinformation disclosed by Gloucester's sight has led to his downfall. Correlating to their experience, the *New Testament* advises one to "pull out," or eradicate, the offending part if one is to rid himself of the "mote" that blinds him ("Matthew," 7:3-5).

Lear and Gloucester, the characters in the play who occupy the most responsible positions as fathers and rulers of their respective families and dominions, are the characters whose judgments bear most weight; and they are, therefore, the ones who are afflicted with the greatest pain for their errors. Their judgments are consequential because of their power and authority; hence, they suffer more than the other characters. Both are undone because of their "follies," and both become wise when they are exposed "to feel what wretches feel." Both have been placed in jeopardy by their "offices," their positions of authority; and just because they have wielded dominion over others, they become the tragic victims of their own mistakes. Ironically, it is only after they have been stripped of authority and have become powerless that they realize their former responsibilities and errors. They become truly sympathetic human beings only after they have been deprived of the authority and the faculties most responsible for their follies. Paralleling Lear's lines:

> Poor naked wretches, wheresoe'er you are,
> That bide the pelting of this pitiless storm,
> How shall your houseless heads and unfed sides,
> Your loop'd and window'd raggedness, defend you
> From seasons such as these? O, I have ta'en
> Too little care of this! Take physic, pomp;
> Expose thyself to feel what wretches feel,
> That thou may'st shake the superflux to them
> And show the heavens more just. (III, iv, 35-43),

is Gloucester's statement:

> . . .that I am wretched
> Makes thee happier. Heavens, deal so still!
> Let the superfluous and lust-dieted man,
> That slaves your ordinance, that will not see
> Because he does not feel, feel your power quickly;
> So distribution should undo excess,
> And each man have enough. (IV, ii, 80-86)

Both protagonists have achieved self-knowledge and compassion through losing what had been most important to them. Ironically, both achieve realization of their responsibilities and the prerequisites for governing well after they have been divested of their authoritative means. At this point in the play, they have become aware of what they were and who they are; yet now they have no power to do anything about it. This development is perhaps the major irony of the play.

Yet, it is also ironical that the other characters in the play frequently appear to be otherwise than they are. The major characters in *King Lear* can be roughly grouped into four distinct categories: the *subjective* sufferers from life—Lear and Gloucester; the *objective* knowers of life—Kent, the Fool, Cordelia, and Edgar; the *active*, self-seeking villains and exploiters—Cornwall, Edmund, Goneril, and Regan; and the passive, selfless, virtuous characters—Edgar, Albany, and Cordelia.

King Lear and Gloucester are the suffering victims of the illusions, or appearances, initiated by the active, evil individuals in the play. Lear and Gloucester appear as the proper symbols for suffering, erring man, who is subject to mistaken notions during most of his earthly existence, who mistakenly regards his responsibilities as privileges and personal benefits, and who unwittingly undermines himself by seeking to exalt himself. Both Lear and Gloucester, like mankind generally, suffer because they lack self-knowledge and are consequently ignorant of their world and their true responsibilities. They are unconsciously the victims of their self-imposed delusions. Man's plight similarly results from his delusions—delusions upon which he make himself dependent and which he acknowledges as truths. Herein lies the grotesquely comic predicament of man, who, always acting in ignorance, brings about his own misery. The profound truth elucidated by *King Lear* is that man's evey act is at once tragic and comic: tragic, because man suffers for his actions; comic, because he acts in the anticipation of fulfilling his desires and is almost always frustrated. He does not know what he is doing, but he thinks he does; therein lies the comedy of his situation. As Gloucester ultimately realizes,

> As flies to wanton boys are we to the gods;
> They kill us for their sport. (IV, i, 36-37)

But the suffering which ensues from man's ignorant actions provides his predicament also with tragedy.

Subjectivity is, or course, Lear's tragic flaw. He is unable to see things as they are but instead sees them as he wants them to be. Because Cordelia and Kent do not say what he wants to hear, they are exiled. The ordinary man employs the same technique: what he does not want to acknowledge, he banishes or alienates from his consciousness. Later in the play, Lear interprets Edgar's simulated madness in terms of his own aberration. Surely two ungrateful daughters brought Edgar to this state (III, ii, 55, 68-69, 75-80). Even in his invective to the storm he is subjective. He considers the storm's pitiless ventings as a personal affront to him (III, ii, 14-24). Lear's lack of objectivity, his inability to laugh as himself, is the source of his tragedy; a sense of self-directed humor would have saved Lear's sanity.

Both protagonists are in an ironic situation; for though their predicaments excite pity, they are essentially comic figures who receive what they deserve. One symathizes with them only because their subjectivity is a flaw common to all men. The appeal of *King Lear* resides in the fact that it deals, in a sense, with every man's tragedy.

Lear, like Hamlet, Othello, and Macbeth, is indeed isolated from his fellowmen; but unlike the others, not because of any superiority. Whereas other protagonists are objectively superior and hence *really* tragic, Lear only believes himself so. His pre-eminence is conveyed by his office as king; he does not possess intrinsic superiority. Hamlet, Othello, and Macbeth are not in communion with other characters because of an inherent nobility, or a greatness, that necessitates tragic isolation; but Lear is *incommunicado,* not because others fail to understand him, but because he is unable to understand them.

Lear, because his superiority is only nominal, is not objectively worthy of tragic treatment. A sympathetic attitude towards Lear's suffering is achieved only by affiliating his subjective posture to one's own. W. H. Clemen points out,

> . . . the very first scene gives us a hint of how Lear is going to lose contact with his natural relation to his environment. The dialogue which he carries on with his daughters is at bottom not a true dialogue, that is, a dialogue based on a mutual understanding. Lear determines in advance the answers he will receive; he fails to adapt himself to the person with whom he is speaking. Hence his complete and almost incomprehensible misunderstanding of Cordelia. . . .

> . . .Lear gazes within himself; he no longer sees people nor what goes on about him. In madness a man is alone with himself; he speaks more to his own person than to others; where he does not

speak to himself, he creates for himself a new and
imaginary partner. . . .[54]

Clemen has, I believe, discerned the most salient point in Lear's
tragedy—the fact that he enjoys no communion with humanity. This
characteristic is, of course, common to many of Shakespeare's
protagonists; but in this case, the lack of communication is not
humanity's fault, but entirely the fault of the protagonist. Lear is well
understood by the other characters, but he fails to understand them; he
has fabricated his own world and expects others to do and say what he
desires of them. Ironically then, the tragedy portrayed is self-created by
the protagonist and is enacted in his own consciousness. Only by
becoming a part of Lear's subjective universe can one participate in his
tragic experience.

Thus, one may conclude that Lear and Gloucester, of all the
characters in the Lear universe, best exemplify the ironic plight of the
ordinary man; their tragedies peculiarly arouse sympathy in the dramatic
spectator, for he recognizes in them his own helplessness and his own
follies. In a sense, both the protagonists and the spectator are the
victims of a reality which they are unable to understand or to cope with.

To emphasize Lear's and Gloucester's inability to see things as they
are, as well as to supply needed equipoise, Shakespeare employs the
ironic provision of four characters who serve as objective foils to the
protagonists' subjectivity. These characters, the truth-speakers—Kent,
the Fool, Cordelia, and Edgar—are aware of the true nature of the
protagonists as well as the natures of the other characters. They render
rather unwelcome service by correcting and checking the illusive
projects fancied by the protagonists.

Kent's distrust of appearances is intimated in the first scene and is
fully brought out later in the play. At its beginning, he is Lear's most
trusted counselor, one who understands Lear's deficiencies but serves
him loyally nevertheless. He provides the objectivity, which Lear sorely
lacks, in appraising the affairs of state. Recognizing Lear's folly in
dividing the kingdom and especially his error in conferring power to the
wrong people, he evinces a complete disregard for his own safety and
well-being when he dares to cross the splenetic old king (I, i, 152-163;
165-68; 169-170; 171-172; 176-79). Unlike Lear, he recognizes his
responsibility and will not be deterred from fulfilling it. He has no
pretensions, no ambitions for advancement, no ilusions about himself.
He knows himself and his purpose in life. Completely dedicated to his
life task, which is loyally to serve the king and the best interests of the

---

[54]W. H. Clemen, *op. cit.*, pp. 134-35.

kingdom, he does these services even when he is out of favor with both the crown and the state.

> My life I never held but as a pawn
> To wage against thine enemies, nor fear to lose it,
> Thy safety being motive. (I, i, 166-68)

> See better, Lear, and let me still remain
> The true blank of thine eye. (I, i, 169-170)

And though his loyalty is ironically judged treasonous by Lear, he does not alter his purpose of serving his master. His virtue is an honesty that unquestioningly and simply accepts its role in life without aspiring to be other than what it is.

The Fool, like Kent, provides objectivity to Lear, but in another capacity. Whereas Kent apprizes Lear of the truth in political matters, the Fool reveals to Lear the truth about himself. As Kent correctly understands the nature of Lear's political responsibilities, so the Fool accurately diagnoses the nature of Lear's own person and provides Lear with the mirror whereby he may see himself. Though Lear often does not appreciably benefit from the Fool's revelations, they are made nevertheless. Subconsciously, at least, Lear recognizes his need for the Fool. This need is especially apparent when Lear is slighted at Goneril's palace where it appears to him that "the world's asleep" (it heeds not his wishes). Here he seeks the objective balm of the Fool. The Fool's objective rendition of Lear's subjective discomfiture fortifies the old king when the external world poses its trying contradictions to his subjective self-illusions. The Fool comforts Lear when the latter's wishes are contradicted at Goneril's palace, then at Gloucester's castle, and finally on the heath during the storm. As long as the Fool is with him, Lear retains a measure of sanity. When the Fool leaves him, Lear is bereft of what little objective balance he had and becomes totally divorced from reality and succumbs to madness.

Curiously, the Fool's manner of speech intimates his role in the drama, as Kent's does to a lesser extent; the Fool's function is to be spokesman for the unadorned truth. He never employs blank verse, nor does he employ the "conventional, measured and dignified manner of speech"[55] used by most of the characters. In contrast to Lear, the Fool uses little decoration in his language; his speech has no poetical embellishments except those which are accidental. Though the speech of the Fool is replete with animal imagery, gnomic wisdom, simple logic, and song, his diction sparingly employs alliteration, similes,

---

[55]*Ibid.*, p. 141.

onomatopoeia, or metaphors; for these are devices of rhetoric which appeal to the imagination or emotions rather than the intellect. As commentator, or chorus, he speaks in prose, the language of fact, rather than in blank verse, the language of emotion. His speech is full of such elliptical devices as aphaeresis, apocope, and syncope, all of which show an ill regard for beautified or decorative language. He is concerned with the truth rather than the exaltation of the emotions. The rhetorical devices most employed by the Fool are summary, contrast and paradox, and argument and persuasion. All are devices utilized by one who is making an appeal to the reason rather than to the emotions. His use of metabasis and epiphonema illustrates his concern with truth; invariably, he summarizes Lear's experience in terms that strip the passions and emotions from it. Lear's heart-rending misery becomes material for comedy when the Fool critically epitomizes Lear's grief in its essential comic aspect. Observe in the following speech his ironic use of metabasis to articulate the utter absurdity of Lear's banishing Cordelia:

> Why this fellow hath banish'd two on's
> daughters, and did the third a blessing
> against his will. If thou follow him, thou
> must needs wear my coxcomb. (I, iv, 113-117)

The very acts that have made Lear miserable, his banishment of Cordelia and his establishment of Goneril and Regan as joint rulers of England, are summarized by the Fool as being comic. According to the Fool, Lear has ironically and foolishly done the opposite of what he intended: he has banished, not Cordelia, who still loves him, but Regan and Goneril, who are more distant from Lear in love than their sister. Cordelia, whom he had intended to punish, has instead been blessed, for she is removed from his foolish authority. Only a fool would follow Lear.

The Fool, while he is perhaps not the only character in the play objective enough to realize the ironic nature of human existence, is the only one whose every utterance throbs this implicit refrain. Recognizing the ironic substratum inherent in every act, he generalizes the truth resident in each particular event. Through the use of epiphonema, the Fool points out this paradoxical nature of existence and the absurd interpretations subjectively imposed upon life in his ironic rejoinder to Lear's pathetic statement: "O me, my rising heart! but, down!" (II, iv, 122). With cruel humor the Fool advises the suffering Lear to

> Cry to it, nuncle, as the cockney did to the eels
> when she put 'em i' the paste alive; she knapp'd
> 'em o' the coxcombs with a stick, and cried 'Down,
> wantons, down!' 'T was her brother that, in pure

kindness to his horse, buttered his hay. (II, iv, 123-26)

Once again the Fool illustrates, this time through a parabolic summary, Lear's own ridiculously tragic plight. He implies that Lear's suffering is of his own making, that his own subjectivity has wrought his suffering.

The Fool, because he always conveys the comic aspect of Lear's tragedy, has a salubrious effect on Lear. Using the rhetorical device of antithesis, he tells Lear:

> I have used it, nuncle, ever since thou mad'st
> thy daughters thy mother; for when thou gav'st
> them the rod, and put'st down thy own breeches,
> (Singing) Then they for sudden joy did weep,
> And I for sorrow sung,
> That such a king should play bo-peep,
> And go the fools among.
>
> (I, iv, 169-75)

Again the Fool uses irony and the juxtaposition of incongruities to depict Lear truly. By relinquishing his position of paternal authority and conferring his prerogatives and powers to his daughters, Lear has become, in a sense, their child instead of their father. They weep for joy, and the Fool sings for sorrow, paradoxical proceedings consequent to the incongruities of Lear's ironic act.

Through his songs, his proverbs, and his paradoxical utterances, the Fool, besides making obvious the absurdity of Lear's tragedy, ironically portrays the nature of Lear's predicament. But more than that, he depicts the precarious situation of all men, who, because of their subjectivity, are unable to see themselves and the world as they really are. No man is able to view his "own crucifixion and bloody crowning" with a separate eye. Man's tragedy, the result of his essentially subjective nature, causes him pain while it produces comedy for those who merely observe the absurdities of his actions and pretensions.

Critics, such as Nahum Tate[56] and Leo Tolstoy,[57] who regard the Fool as a superfluous character in the tragedy of *King Lear,* seem to

---

[56]Nahum Tate in his revision of *King Lear* (1687) excludes the Fool from his cast of characters as well as perpetrating other artistic atrocities even more egregious.

[57]Leo Tolstoy in his article "On Shakespeare and the Drama," *Fortnightly Review,* LXXXVI (1906), 963-83, speaks of the 'senseless words' of the Fool and sees no significant function for the Fool in the play. He also considers Edmund, Gloucester, and Edgar (the whole Gloucester plot, in fact) to be unnecessary and distracting.

miss the main point of the play. The double-faced nature of man's proceedings is delineated by Shakespeare's use of the Fool to present the objective, comic view of human life; while Lear, in contrast, provides the subjective, tragic point of view. Lear has his fool, and the Fool has his—Lear. It is the Fool who, more than any other character, makes one aware of the cruel humor which underlies tragedy.

Cordelia, like Kent and the Fool, provides objectivity to Lear. There are three domains over which King Lear wields controlling power: himself, the state, and his family. And Lear, although he doesn't realize it, has an indissoluble relationship to three characters who are indispensable to the integrity of these three domains; these three—Kent, the Fool, and Cordelia—are all notable for their bluntness in telling Lear the truth. Just as the Fool is indispensable to Lear's sanity and Kent is essential to political stability, so Cordelia is necessary to his domestic integrity. Just as the Fool and Kent give stability to Lear's status as King and person, so Cordelia validates his paternal function.

When the play begins, Lear does not realize that these three persons are integral to his well-being, security, and health. He believes himself entirely self-sufficient, "ague-proof." But he does not know himself, nor does he know how intrinsic is the bond that ties him to others. Consequently he banishes from him two of those individuals whose lives are as much dependent upon him as his is upon them. Because Kent and Cordelia bluntly speak the truth in terms that seem to "pale" his deluded self-image, Lear attempts to "cancel and tear to pieces that great bond" between himself and them which actually nurtures his royalty and authority. Significantly, the Fool is not present when Lear banishes Cordelia and Kent. Since the Fool supplies self-integrity, Lear appropriately is not wholly himself when the Fool is absent. Lear's terrible misjudgment takes place because he does not know how closely intertwined is the knot between himself and these three characters; so intrinsic is this knot that only death can ultimately dissolve it. The banishment of Kent and Cordelia is an indication of the fact that Lear is death-bound. When he disinherits Cordelia, his family begins to disintegrate; when he banishes Kent, his kingdom collapses; and when the Fool departs, his personality falls apart. Without them, Lear is "an O without a figure," a pathetic semblance of his former self. After Kent and Cordelia are banished, the Fool tells Lear who he is: "Lear's shadow" (I, iv, 251).

Unlike the subjective Lear, these three knowers of the truth realize the indissoluble bond between themselves and Lear. Cordelia serves Lear even after banishment by returning from France to take care of him and to restore to him his divided kingdom. Kent also, after having been banished, still follows and serves his lord disguised as the humble Caius, attending upon Lear in a meaner capacity while still attempting to preserve at least the semblance of authority in the now powerless and defunct king. The Fool follows and attends upon Lear, though no longer bound to do so, serving one who "is out of favor." The fortunes of these three rise and fall with Lear's. With the Fool's departure, Lear becomes forgetful of who he is; *i. e.*, he has lost personal identity. With Cordelia's death comes the end of Lear's family. And when Lear dies, Kent prepares to follow:

> I have a journey, sir, shortly to go.
> My master calls me; I must not say no.
> (V, iii, 321-22)

Lear's self-inflicted sufferings, then, derive from his failure to recognize his dependency upon others and the inviolable bond existing between himself and those who truly serve him. His condition, denoting as it does the general malaise of human existence, cannot but elicit sympathy from a responsive audience. His tragedy, like ours, stems from the estrangement of himself from others. And we, like Lear, by disbranching ourselves from our "material sap," must "come to deadly use." Left to himself and his devices, Lear is a helpless, absurd figure, a shadow of what he should be. His position in the world is defined and given meaning only insofar as he identifies with others. When "the bond is crack'd," everything that truly denotes him disintegrates: his authority, his kingdom, his family, even his identity.

As Kent, the Fool, and Cordelia are to Lear, so Edgar is to Gloucester. Just as Lear's fortunes decline when these three characters leave him, so Gloucester's worldly position and personal welfare diminish after he repudiates Edgar. When Gloucester does not listen to Edgar (he does not even give Edgar a hearing) and instead hearkens to the maleficent Edmund, he unwittingly brings catastrophe upon himself. Like Cordelia, whom he much resembles, Edgar makes no effort to defend himself when he is maligned. Also like her, he is as indispensable to his father's well-being as she is to hers; for when Edgar leaves his father's household, Edmund begins to accomplish Gloucester's ruination.

Just as the disguised Kent, unbeknown to his deranged master, had rendered service to his king, so Edgar, also disguised, provides succor to the father who had disowned him. After Gloucester has been blinded, Edgar, in the guises of a bedlam beggar and a rustic peasant, directs and advises his father. His simulated madness much resembles the wise "absurdities" of the Fool. Edgar, accordingly then, incorporates the same qualities that were noted in Cordelia, Kent, and the Fool, and he functions similarly in the play.[58]

Lear and Gloucester ironically brought destruction to themselves by rejecting *legitimacy; i. e.,* by banishing the truth in favor of self-vaunting flattery. By asserting their self-sufficiency and their independence from others, they unwittingly estranged themselves from amity and prosperity. The egocentricity of Lear and Gloucester and its destructive qualities are personified by the *illegitimate* persons in the play: Regan, Goneril, and Edmund. The theme of illegitimacy pervades the whole play. The "loners"—Regan, Goneril, and Edmund—are self-seekers (as are Lear and Gloucester, in another sense of the word), who are trying to establish their identities ironically through divorcing themselves from their responsibilities to those who engendered them. Regan, Goneril, and Edmund not only deny their humanitarian bond, but also assert their independence and individuality by disclaiming the bond of love which should exist between them and their fathers. The effect of this negation is remarked by Albany, as he says to Goneril,

> That nature which contemns its origin
> Cannot be bordered certain in itself.
> She that herself will sliver and disbranch
> From her material sap, perforce must wither
> And come to deadly use. (IV, ii, 32-36)

Ironically, in their attempts to distinguish themselves from others through self-aggrandizement, the three "degenerate bastards" bring death and self-annihilation. Seeking to assert self, they destroy themselves. They die as they have lived, separately and alone. And since they have denied the human bond that confers communion with their race as well as self-validation, they never become truly human. Hence, the animal imagery of the play. Inhuman as they are, their deaths cause no great stir among those who remain alive. Edmund's death, for example, when announced, receives no lamentation; Albany says, "That's but a trifle here." Nor do the deaths of Regan and Goneril elicit any expression of grief:

---

[58]Hugh Maclean's article, "Disguise in *King Lear:* Kent and Edgar," *Shakespeare Quarterly,* II (1960), 49-54, provides an interesting study comparing Kent's and Edgar's use of disguise to find 'the appropriate path through a dangerous world.' Edgar, according to Maclean, properly employs disguise by combining 'knowledge and action' to bring 'order out of chaos,' whereas Kent, in contrast, is vague about his purposes and therefore never achieves 'ripeness' but 'devotes himself primarily to shoring up a ruin.'

Another interesting treatment of Edgar's role in the play is offered by J. T. McCullen's essay, "Edgar: The Wise Bedlam," in *Shakespeare in the Southwest: Some New Directions,* I, edited by T. J. Stafford (El Paso: Texas Western Press, 1969), 43-55. Professor McCullen demonstrates that it is Edgar who brings both Lear and Gloucester to self-realization and to the acceptance of reality.

Kent: Your eldest daughters have fordone
themselves, and desperately are
dead.
Lear: Ay, so I think. (V, iii, 291-93)

By attempting to advance themselves at the expense of others, Regan, Goneril, and Edmund have actually depreciated themselves. They have ironically accomplished the opposite of what they intended. By capitalizing upon the errors of Gloucester and Lear, they have wrought destruction but achieved nothing constructive.

These three, along with Cornwall, comprise the third category of characters. Significantly, the machinations of these vicious characters, for the main part, are most successfully accomplished during the night. They are "night-prowlers" who prey most effectively upon Lear and Gloucester when the protagonists are themselves "in the dark," *i. e.*, in a state of ignorance. The darkness and light imagery permeates *King Lear* with symbolic implications about the characters and their predicaments. Robert Bechtol Heilman, discussing the light and darkness imagery which prevails in the drama, notes that there are characters—Edmund, Goneril, Regan, and Cornwall—who operate best in the dark.[59] This darkness, or ignorance, serves them well in the attainment of their evil goals. Lear and Gloucester, who are "in the dark" about themselves and the world, are perfect dupes for these nocturnal operators.

These "evil" characters, having no real relish of virtue, repeatedly employ virtuous terms and appearances to cloak their vicious intentions. Gloucester and Lear, ignorantly unable to distinguish real virtue from pretended virtue, are the primary victims of these dark predators, who habitually exploit others under the guise of hypocritical virtue. The inherent irony of the human scene avouches the hypocrisy of these characters, who consistently represent themselves as being better than they are. Edmund, of course, knows that he is illegitimate; and Lear, when he learns the true natures of Goneril and Regan, appropriately dubs them "degenerate bastards." A sense of illegitimacy always undergirds the hypocritical posture; for the appearance assumed by the hypocrite invariably belies his true nature, glosses his authentic self; what he pretends to be is not what he is. Such people thrive upon those who are ignorant of reality—and since they have to "make" something of themselves, they are the engineers of action both in drama and in life. They make things happen.

[59]Robert Bechtol Heilman, *This Great Stage: Image and Structure in King Lear* (Baton Rouge: Louisiana State University Press, 1948), pp. 45-46.

W. H. Clemen observes further that these characters, though they may speak fairly, never become sympathetically involved in the lives of others.[60] Their language, however fair, is never rich in imagery; for, wanting imagination, they are unable to respond emotionally to the suffering of the protagonists or the other characters. Instead, they are actively concerned with the event rather than its emotional significance.

Conversely, the virtuous characters, especially Edgar and Cordelia, instead of initiating action, seem rather passive in the play. Often victimized by the vicious agents of evil, they too frequently are spuriously misrepresented or placed in an unfavorable light by the false characters. Unlike the evildoers, they seldom defend themselves (a fact which offends some critics as being implausible; these pundits seem to forget that Christ offered no testimony in his own behalf when He was brought to trial). I do not believe that Cordelia's and Edgar's passivity is the result of what Roy Battenhouse calls Edgar's "pliable weakness of will" and Cordelia's "stubborn will," both alike symptomatic of a "foolish self-defensiveness. . . , a futile shadowboxing which misrepresents to the father the true nature of the child, and thereby provokes in the father a rage and retaliation."[61] On the contrary, I see in neither signs of self-defensiveness. Self-assertive "virtue," we have already discovered, is very probably not virtue; for true merit, always conditioned by ironic self-knowledge, tends to understate itself. A certain litotic *pudeur* prohibits the virtuous person from flaunting that which validates and sanctifies him; informed by ironic wisdom, he knows that those who are not virtuous will traduce and demean the sanctity of truth if it is nakedly exhibited. Assured of their validity, their legitimacy, and resting secure in faithful self-knowledge, Cordelia and Edgar accept the conditions of life as they are, seeking in no way to defend, augment, or re-create themselves. Further, they realize that under no conditions can they create in others a virtue by preaching their own. Therefore, Cordelia "loves and keeps silent," and Edgar removes himself from the unjustified wrath of his father, sure that "some villain hath done me wrong." Knowing further that knowledge and self-illumination cannot be taught, they realize that Lear and Gloucester, if they achieve such knowledge, must do so through the purgative process of suffering. These, it appears to me, are their reasons for keeping silent and not defending themselves.

Thus "with all-unable pen" I have grouped the major characters of *King Lear* into four categories to make apparent the ironic interplay of

[60]W. H. Clemen, *op. cit.*, pp. 134-35.

[61]Battenhouse, *Shakespearean Tragedy: Its Art and Its Christian Premises,* p. 295.

the basic personality types that chiefly exemplify human life in this play.[62] The *objective* group is at odds with the *subjective* group of characters, just as the *active* are opposed to the *passive;* but this dichotomous arrangement, while it obviously estranges the separate groups, also, ironically, brings them together in complementary fashion. While they seem oppositely disposed and antagonistic to each other from the partisan point of view, the ironic perspective sees them not only as inimical but as mutually interdependent. There is commutuality as well as enmity reflected in these character types, a condition that expresses the inherent irony of life. Life depends upon such dichotomies in order to manifest itself.

In *King Lear*, Shakespeare, though he presents the complexity of life, takes no partisan stance and makes no promises. Both virtue and vice are indiscriminately punished and rewarded; Shakespeare's sun shines on "both the just and unjust." For humanity at large, the purpose of life, if it has one, seems mainly educational. Through suffering and experience, man may achieve self-understanding and knowledge. At best, he can perhaps attain the ironic attitude, whereby he can transcend himself and, with one foot beyond life, laugh at his own tragedy.

---

[62]William R. Elton in his *King Lear and the Gods* has grouped the major characters—those comprising the Gloucester and Lear families—according to their exemplifications of the four main religious alternatives ascribed to pagans during the Renaissance: (1) the *priscia theologia,* including Edgar and Cordelia; (2) the atheistic outlook, represented by Goneril, Regan, and Edmund; (3) the superstitious or paganistic view, exemplified by Gloucester; and (4) *deus absconditus,* illustrated by King Lear. Elton's interesting, but exhaustive, consideration of these characters and their exemplary experiences culminates with the thesis that *King Lear,* "an ostensibly 'realistic' depiction of pagan life"—conditioned, however, by the Christian premises of a Jacobean audience—syncretically, through pagan religious analogies, addresses the theological crisis of early seventeenth-century England.

CHAPTER VII

THE THERAPEUTIC EFFECT OF IRONIC DRAMA

All types of drama, I suppose, if they are successful in their intent and if they are well received, do us some good. If they did not, in some way, answer our human needs, we would not attend them with such enthusiasm as we do. Most dramas supply some sort of balm to our hurt minds and souls or minister to the wounds inflicted by life.

Certainly, comedy in its various forms, though it may fail to correct our aims and our ideals, at least relaxes our bent bows and consoles us by exposing the absurd targets that our ill-directed arrows of aspiration have missed or sometimes unfortunately have hit. Comedy, at all events, lets "the air out of our tires" by deflating our pompous egos. It makes us aware of our ultimate unimportance, enables us to laugh at ourselves and our pretensions, and thereby alleviates the tensions of life. Temporarily, at least, we are relieved from the over-fraught anxieties we feel about ourselves, as we view the misadventures of others even less competent and more absurd than we. So it does us good.

Tragedy, on the other hand, absorbs us into the sufferings of its protagonist. Instead of detaching ourselves from his misadventures and laughing, as we did in comedy, at his absurd self-importance, we identify with him. Our sympathetic capacities are aroused in his behalf. By identifying ourselves with him, by sharing his troubles and miseries, we take upon us his peculiar emotional perplexities. But curiously, even in tragedy, we are still able to congratulate ourselves when the play ends, while the unhappy protagonist has expired in agony. For even though we have suffered with him in his extremity of passion, we by-pass the catastrophe which falls on him alone. And so again, as was the case after having viewed comedy, we leave the theater feeling good about ourselves, for we have escaped the calamity that the tragic protagonist succumbed to. Both tragedy and comedy, though methodically opposite, have accomplished similar results. Both experiences have left us feeling intact; we feel relieved that we have experienced yet escaped the absurdities of the one and the miseries of the other.

Both experiences, though they bring a measure of awareness to us, leave us relatively unscathed. Why is this so? There are two main reasons why we who have witnessed the ordeals and perplexities of the two protagonists feel ourselves unimpaired by their misfortunes. The first, obviously, is that we are not they. We are merely spectators, holding ourselves aloof from the dramatic arena where they are the principals. However interested we may have been in their affairs, their tussels with life are not ours. We are not the victims, as they are, of their particular illusions, frustrations, and mistakes. We, as spectators, are in the *know;* we perceive their errors; we recognize their limitations; we are sufficiently detached from their problems to gauge their behavior as it relates to their world; we see the dramatic context in which they operate.

The second reason why we feel ourselves exonerated from the dilemma that has frustrated them is that our commitment to their world was not total. When we observed the comedy, we directed only our intellectual and critical faculties to its spectacle. Suspending our moral and emotional functions, we regaled our senses and our mind at their expense. We came to the theater prepared for laughter, not for tears.

Conversely, when we observed the tragedy, we subjectively identified with the suffering protagonist by alerting our sympathy and compassion. We focused our attention upon his calamity, commiserating with him and suspending our moral and intellectual percipience in favor of our emotional receptivity. Consequently, we were oblivious to the comic content of the protagonist's dilemma.

In the comedy, however, there was fodder for tragedy, if we had been disposed to find it. If we had *subjectively* viewed the protagonist's frustrations, we would have wept rather than laughed at his misadventures. If we had *objectively* observed the tragedy, we would have found adequate "store of provender" for laughter. What, after all, is more absurd than a self-important human being who querulously asserts himself and his dignity against forces that will inevitably reduce him to a "handful of dust"?

It must be apparent now that the effect of comedy or tragedy depends not only upon its author's intention and his competence, but also upon the disposition and the development of the spectator's cognitive functions. However serious the tragedy, it brushes the truth of life closely enough to absorb at least some trace of comic potential; and, likewise, however farcical or frivolous the comedy, enough residual seriousness clings from its lightsome contact with reality to provoke a tear. Neither form really intends a realistic rendering of life, but rather focuses upon a single aspect of the human experience; as a result, both tragedy and comedy fail to address the total man. Neither dramatic vehicle affords a balanced view of life nor a faithful representation of reality.

The morality, the miracle, and the mystery plays afford insight into man's moral predicament. But again, like the comedy and the tragedy, these plays address only an aspect of man's whole nature; and, like the tragedy and the comedy, they effect only partial edification. Moral development, though certainly praiseworthy, hardly supplies man with the salvific experience he requires. Doubtless, it increases his moral awareness, but it does not embrace the whole complex nature of human life. Since man is not simply a moral agent, to develop this facet of his nature at the expense of his other cognitive faculties is to distort him into a religious bigot or fanatic. Yet the morality, miracle, and mystery plays, like tragedies and comedies, if they are well presented and rightly received, make us feel good.

The chronicle play, too, may have salutary effects. For the chronicle play, besides arousing patriotic fervor and exciting admiration for historical worthies, stimulates man's will to accomplish notable feats and perform memorable tasks. By commemorating man's achievements, it, like the tragedy, supplies a sense of dignity and worth to the human enterprise. But like the other dramatic forms, it fails to address the whole self, concentrating instead upon man's history; and, like the others, it makes us feel good about ourselves as we leave the theater.

Thus, we see that all the dramatic forms existing in Shakespeare's day were unable separately to effect a veritable representation of human life. And while each dramatic type gratified some single human faculty, it failed to supply the integral view of life which leads to self-fulfillment.

Such, in brief, are the limitations that one observes when he considers the *pure* forms of the dramatic genres popular during the English Renaissance. The truth is, of course, that Elizabethan drama was not purely tragic or comic or historical or moral; the vitality of the age precluded that possibility. The profuse enthusiasm for variety and novelty, which almost characterizes the age, was reflected in the rich confusion of Elizabethan dramaturgy. Only the most audacious pedantry could presume to classify Shakespeare's plays into the three simple categories of comedy, history, and tragedy. At best, such classification is artificial and misleading. Shakespeare's comedies, implicitly when not openly, included material fit for tragedy; and it was his habit frequently to interpose and mix serious incidents with his comic scenes. Interspersed throughout his chronicle plays, one finds both comic and tragic potentiality.

But the point I wish to make is this: Shakespeare had tended throughout his dramatic career toward composite drama, a type of play that would unify and harmonize his own dramatic inclinations and the various dramatic proclivities of his age. As his vision of life expanded and as his dramatic experience deepened, he accomplished in *King Lear*, not only a composite drama, but a dramatic stance that transcended the partisan efforts of his contemporaries—a cosmic outlook that "damn'd," their dramatic endeavors, "like an ill-roasted egg, all on one side."

The dramatic view which *King Lear* exemplifies I have called *ironic*. I have used the term *ironic* to describe the particular view of life which embraces, as it harmonizes, all the discordant incongruities spawned by the lavish, creative life impulse. Applied to drama, it is a view that repudiates the strictures of classical drama—its unity, its simplicity of structure, its orderliness, its purity, and its freedom from excess. Attic drama, for all its reputed splendor and artistic precision, does not yield a faithful picture of human life.

Aristotle's *Poetics* designated tragedy the highest form of literature, and for nearly 2500 years hardly anyone has raised a dissenting voice. But in spite of my veneration for Aristotle and the accomplishments of the Greeks, I cannot, in view of subsequent literary and dramatic developments, wholly acquiesce to Aristotle's opinion. To do so would, in fact, be tantamount to denying not only the evolution and the progress attained through subsequent literary endeavors, but also the creative, dynamic nature of life itself. The cultural and social changes occurring during the last 2500 years preclude the validity of such a categorical conclusion. While I willingly acknowledge that Greek tragedy has not been eclipsed, nor even equalled, by the tragic drama written by any people of any other era, I question the contention that it is the highest form of literature for all people during all ages. One might even question, as well, the plausibility of applying the Attic conception of tragedy to subsequent literature, since the latter arises from cultural, social, religious, and political circumstances radically different from those which occasioned the Greek conception of life. The tragic conception, I am thinking , might very well be a peculiarly Hellenistic attitude to the dilemma of man. Certainly, the neoclassical efforts of the seventeenth and eighteenth centuries to emulate Greek tragedy and to reproduce the Attic attitude cannot but strike us as being highly artificial; their pseudo-tragedies seem mere contrivances of a society whose world outlook diverged drastically from that of the ancient Greeks. Any attempt to resuscitate or duplicate the tragic perspective expressed in the plays of Aeschylus, Sophocles, and Euripides is bound to fall short, as the ambitious failures of the neo-classicists pathetically demonstrate. Tragedy, after all, was the dramatic forte of the ancient Greek playwrights; no one has written better tragedies than they, for no other age has produced the conditions or the conventions that would uphold such a perspective of life as their tragic writers had.

But the tragic view of life, while it imparts dignity to man's estate, does not survey the whole human experience. It teaches us self-respect and enlarges our capacities to feel; it deepens our emotional response to human experience; but is does not *heal* us from the wounds we sustain in living, for it ignores certain aspects of our human nature. Its focus is too narrow to engage the whole complexity of the human soul. The *catharsis* accomplished by tragedy, though it points us, perhaps, in the right direction, fails to provide the *stasis* which is essential to our psychic well-being. *Catharsis* may "settle" our emotional "stomachs" by purging our emotional "hang-ups" and thus making us feel better, but it does not cure us from the ills of life nor fortify us to deal successfully with them. At best, purgation is only the first step in the therapeutic process.

Then tragedy, like all the other dramatic genres, is essentially palliative, a medicine which ministers only to particular human disorders, or dis-eases, which we have contracted from being alive. Tragedy may well be the most bitter of the pills we have to swallow in order to feel better about ourselves, but comedies, morality plays, and histories also supply other kinds of medication to our psychic sickness.

King Lear, unlike its dramatic predecessors, does not allow an escape route from the dilemmas of life by localizing, then anesthetizing or pacifying a specific human malaise. If not well received and wholesomely responded to, the play may leave us perplexed rather than fortified. Since it addresses, not one or two, but all of our psychic functions, we are almost as much engaged by the multiple significations of its action as we are by the complex hermeneutics of life itself. It admits no relaxation of those cognitive faculties whose inertness would allow a one- or two-dimensional interpretation of the situation at hand; we cannot satisfactorily reduce the dramatic phenomenon to its comic, or tragic, or moral, or historic significance. We cannot, in other words, evade the complexity posed by the dramatic situation; we must, instead, awaken all our sensibilities in order to resolve the cosmic tensions that such a play arouses. By alerting our faculties, the ironic drama then sharpens us to deal with life, since its complexity requires the harmonious interplay of all our human capabilities. It demands, as other plays do not, the integration of our functions and sensibilities, and it yields us, as its fruit, therapeutic conditioning for meaningful living; it educates us for an effective, well-integrated life.

King Lear, as the prototype for ironic drama, defines structurally and thematically the form toward which Shakespeare's later plays had pointed; it presents a formal demonstration of his ironic methodology set forth in graphic outline. The therapeutic result of his ironic method is conditioned by rather radical departures from the dramatic conventions that had prevailed among his predecessors. It differs, as Northrop Frye has observed, from other earlier Shakespearean tragedies by

> . . .the antithesis of tragedy and comedy. . . , and with it the antithesis of creator and creature. The paradox of tragedy, the vision of what is at once natural and absurd, is united to the paradox of comedy, a vision of what is equally natural and absurd in a different context. Here there is neither

a chaos to re-create nor a new community floating away into the land of dreams, but, like the island of *The Tempest* which is Mediterranean and yet so curiously American as well, an old world that is a brave new world, an inheritance of which we are at least the rightful possessors.[63]

Therapeusis, first of all, depends upon the conception of a protagonist who elicits not only our sympathy but our understanding. He must be humanly ordinary enough to allow the audience to identify with him. He must be subject to the same temporal and spiritual limitations that typically restrict human beings. He should not be, as the Greek tragic protagonist usually is, extraordinary or exceptional; his plane of action must be within the ken of the audience, or else full identification cannot occur. Lear and Gloucester are, therefore, excellent examples of the ironic hero in that the audience, despite Lear's and Gloucester's worldly status, has no difficulty in identifying with them. These protagonists are susceptible to the same kinds of errors and illusions that men generally suffer from. It is necessary that the protagonist not have an unusual tragic flaw; such a flaw would isolate him from the audience's understanding.

Furthermore, the ironic protagonist must be flexible. He should not obdurately resist forces less noble than himself, but rather he should succumb to the vicissitudes of life; for if he is not conditioned by the circumstances of life, he is not amenable to correction or instruction and is, therefore, incapable of *therapeusis.* It is the inflexibility, or intransigence, of the tragic protagonist against relentless fate or the inexorable demands of life that eventuates in catastrophe and that excites the fearful wonder of the spectator as he beholds tragedy. As a tragic witness of the spectacle, he is awed and overwhelmed, but not illumined, because he is not "wedded" to the action but merely "engaged" to it. Emotionally he is drained by the experience, left limp, as it were, but not spiritually fortified.

In addition, ironic drama concentrates upon the finite conditions of human life, such conditions as are credible and accessible to universal human experience. While not prohibiting "supernatural solicitings" nor denying the reality of a supermundane order, an ironic play squarely focuses on the actual issues of man's life. Superterrestrial dodges that tempt one to escape the realities of his finite existence are exposed as subjective hallucinations that impede rather than foster spiritual development. A case in point occurs in *Richard II,* where Richard, instead of making a realistic effort to prevent his deposition, evades the

---

[63]Northrop Frye, *Fools of Time* (Toronto: University of Toronto Press, 1967), p.121.

exigencies of his situation by beguiling himself into thinking that God "hath in heavenly pay" glorious angels who will defend Richard's rights. Also debarred in ironic drama are those rarified concepts that promise reward for virtue, punishment for vice, and other idealistic subterfuges that evade the reality of man's finitude. Such subterfuges, since they are not universally validated by human experience, devise escape from the problems that regularly and perenially perplex human beings.

Furthermore, in ironic drama, *anagnorisis*, or revelation, is displaced by *stasis*. *Stasis* chiefly differs from *anagnorisis* in that the former temporally confirms the actual life process, whereas the latter *affirms* detachment or disengagement from the perplexities of life. *Anagnorisis* affirms a delusive certainty about the truth of human existence; the tragic protagonist, it claims, has now achieved self-knowledge and truth. Such an affirmation precludes relapse as well as progress, because it terminates the experience of the tragic protagonist. Released from the relativities of life, he reposes in the truth. *Stasis*, on the other hand, by temporally confirming life, does not close the doors of experience. By *temporal confirmation*, I mean to say that the ironic protagonist, when he attains self-awareness cannot rest *permanently* in his enlightened state. To do so would not only violate the reality of the temporal, finite order, but negate the vitality of experience and deny progress to the life process. *Stasis* provides to the hitherto disoriented individual a stay amidst the warring dichotomies of life, but it is a sanctuary, not a home. At best, it affords a sabbath, a momentary rest in the presence of truth, but it is not a final solution. Since growth and experience are essential to living, absolute certainty and ultimate security would put an end to spiritual growth and terminate the historical process. Lear, thus when he achieves self-awareness, suffers a relapse from the certitude or faith that he has acquired. He experiences spiritual growth and expanded awareness, but he does not rest content, but instead finds himself plunged into further experience that craves ampler knowledge. There are, after all, many mansions that life prepares for human habitation, but in none should we be locked.

Usually accompanying *anagnorisis* in Greek tragedy is *peripeteia*, or reversal of situation. With the revelation or enlightenment attained by the protagonist comes a change in his life style, as he feels bound to repudiate the "errors" of his past life. Note that the Greek tragic assumption is that the protagonist's enlightenment informs him of "the truth," that he is now a *changed* man who accordingly must alter his life's priorities and direction. The old illusions that formerly determined his behavior are therefore renounced in favor of his newly acquired knowledge. Tragedy teaches that one way is better than another, that "knowledge," though belatedly found, is better than the "ignorance," which before had led the protagonist astray. But the protagonist's former "ignorance," the tragic playwright seems to forget, is what put him on the road to "knowledge." And if the path of ignorance, or illusion, has led to knowledge, or truth, is ignorance really an ultimately undesirable condition, or is it not, in fact, simply a station on the road to one's destination? And if the protagonist has truly been enlightened and knows himself now, whereas before he did not, is that not cause for rejoicing rather than lamentation and grief? The recognition of past error or sin need not be a cause for wailing, nor for the drastic catastrophe which the tragic hero invariably brings upon himself. The shame, or sense of guilt, which follows *anagnorisis* and which overwhelms the protagonist with misery, is a sign, not of spiritual growth nor even genuine enlightenment, but of a puffed-up egoist, the so-called "superior" man of Greek tragedy; his overweening self-importance has caused him to excommunicate himself from other men by "cancelling that great bond which," he believes, "keeps" him "pale."

Contrary to the *peripeteia* of Greek tragedy, Shakespeare's *Lear* teaches "a better way." Instead of a renunciation of the old way of life with its errors, misapprehensions, and misjudgments, King Lear, unlike the Greek tragic hero, assimilates his new knowledge in order to establish communion with his fellow man. He noticeably is changed after he discovers that he is not "ague-proof" and that man, despite his pretensions and sophistication, when "unaccommodated" is "a poor, bare, forked animal." Lear's illumination accomplishes forbearance, toleration, and understanding of others; he becomes less self-centered and more concerned with other people and less preoccupied with his own misery. He does not, when he discovers the truth about himself, wreak catastrophic violence, as the tragic hero is wont to do, but rather commences to develop patience, understanding, and tolerance—qualities he had formerly lacked. He does not drastically repudiate the selfishness of his old way of life; in fact, in his infirmity, he relapses at the end of the play into his former subjective habit of construing things as he would desire them to be. But he retains, even in his final madness, the spiritual dimension that he has acquired through his suffering. The "redemption" of past mistakes by graciously making them meaningful to one's present state of awareness is contrary to Aristotle's *peripeteia,* which excludes or repudiates the errors of one's past. The ironic process that integrates the illusive mistakes of the past with present truth I will call *symbiosis.* Where *peripeteia* implies abscission or renunciation of one mode of life for another that is regarded as more authentic, *symbiosis* includes the "falsity" of the past by "harmonizing" it with the present cognizant mode. *Symbiosis* absorbs error, even "transfigures" it, and gives it a place in the living experience of the protagonist. *Symbiosis* allows the various "errors" and "truths" to *live* together in a richly organic commutuality that is experientially prolific rather than narrowly barren and eclectic. Where *peripeteia* poses for the audience an either/or situation, *symbiosis* yields "sunshine and rain at once," transforming sorrow into a "rarity most belov'd." Because

76

symbiosis reconciles opposition and furthers the evolution of variety and diversity, it concurs with the untrammeled process of life much more successfully than does *peripeteia.*

The ironic drama, unlike classical tragedy, admits the intrusion of apparent irrelevancies into its framework. For irrelevancies are the very stuff from which new experience is born. Ironic drama welcomes "every chance into its pot," because the random data, from which life moulds its language, provide the occasions for its creative purpose. Classical tragedy, by forbidding irrelevancies, imposes upon life its own message; it thereby narrows life, forcing upon it strictures that prohibit spontaneity. The seeming irrelevancies of life are, after all, often the "indirections" by which we "find directions out."

Since ironic drama is more concerned with the internal drama unfolding in the spirit of the protagonist than with the happenings of the external world, such "irrelevancies" naturally abound. For the whole tenor of the ironic experience is based upon the incongruities and ambiguities of phenomena. The ironist is not imposed upon by the external event; rather, he regards it as the objective expression of an internal condition. The internal world, or rather the spiritual reality, that undergirds and gives significance to the external event, engages his undivided attention. All events are relevant to him, but only insofar as they express, however ambiguously, the subjective reality that gives them meaning. Paradoxically then, what may at first seem irrelevant can assume pertinence to the ironic drama if it derives from the vital impulse. The true irrelevancies in drama are those events or words that do not communicate life, that are merely conventional trade coins. Mechanical patterns of behavior, empty palaver, drab social amenities, and the dead verbiage that conveys nothing of its speaker—these are "irrelevancies," for they do not bespeak their vital source. They are lifeless forms, though they may very well reflect a society's spiritual paucity. Such dreary social interloping rattles dead bones but in no way serves the purposes of life.

By knitting together the diverse threads that constitute the fabric of human experience, ironic drama weaves the very pattern of life. *King Lear,* the prototype for such drama, pinpoints the basic source of all human suffering; not simply does it paint the terrible ordeal of one extraordinary individual, as tragedy is wont to do. But its protagonists, as I have shown, exemplify all human beings, and the agonies endured by the two ironic principals are not exceptional, terrible though they may seem. Their suffering, as ours, would be more tolerable were it not intensified by their own subjective obsession with it. *Lear* specifies the subjective root from which sprouts all human anxiety and suffering. The play exposes the core of our disorder and disease and achieves an effect which, rather than rendering vicarious purgative relief, elements restoration; or, to use religious terminology, it points the way to personal salvation. Its aim, unlike tragedy's, is salvific rather than purgatorial. Ironic drama indeed achieves purgation, but only incidentally, as an accessory to its therapeutic intention. It does, like tragedy, scour our souls, purging us from our personal emotional perplexities by applying the abrasive instrument of another's suffering and thus anesthetizing the considerable wounds that life has inflicted upon us; but ironic drama also achieves *therapeusis* by graphic enlightenment, showing the way to psychic harmony and self-fulfillment.

Ironic drama, in regard to its purgative aspect, does not employ the tragic method of *catharsis*, which implements purgation by intensifying misery until it reaches its breaking point, and thereby shattering the protagonist's self-image without removing his self-centeredness. Ironic drama, on the other hand, dissipates emotional intensity by the protagonist's turning from his individual agony long enough to realize that his personal suffering is only an index to the world's suffering.[64] He, unlike the tragic protagonist, identifies with others and feels with "poor naked wretches, wheresoe'er" they "are." He now "sees feelingly." This is crucially different from the tragic experience, for through identifying with others, the ironic protagonist acknowledges the bond between himself and his fellowmen. A communion with mankind ensues; this communion denotes a healing of the breach which had separated him from others. Because the tragic protagonist solipsistically sees himself as the focal center of life, as one set apart from others, he does not receive the benefits of *therapeusis;* broken by life, he remains to the end of the drama insensitive to the sufferings of others. He feels that he was "tripped up," or even "tricked," by the gods or ineluctable fate. The truth he discovers is a disabling truth, for he has not *yet* realized that his is not a special case.

The "better way" to which *therapeusis* points involves a risk of what the unjust world calls madness, as Horowitz has pointed out,[65] for to "see feelingly" is to heal the breach between ourselves and others. To do so entails self-abnegation and an "other-directedness" that contradict the very foundations of the institutions that have sustained Western man's individualistic self-sufficiency and the proud heroism upon which his "tragic dignity" rests. But the "redemption of man's social misery. . rests upon the restoration of human order, based on feeling sight, on the

---

[64]Technically, the ironic dramatist dissipates the audience's over-involvement with the protagonist by distracting it with comic intrusion or by turning the play's focus to another character or to subsidiary actions or interests.

[65]David Horowitz, *Shakespeare: An Existential View* (New York: Hill and Wang, 1965), p. 129.

'compunctious visitings of Nature', in essence, on a return to human kindness."[66]

It is important to note that Lear as a *tragic* protagonist experiences *only* personal suffering; he is hardly cognizant of others' sufferings; Gloucester's blinding and his attempted suicide, Edgar's expulsion and beggary, Kent's and Cordelia's pains of exile—all these miseries endured by others hardly come to Lear's attention. They are subsidiary sufferings, just as poignant as Lear's, but miseries that do not register upon his consciousness because he is too involved in himself and his personal sorrows to give thought to others. This is the typical *tragic* experience; its cathartic effect induces only purgation.

The ironic experience, on the other hand, since it directs one's attention to the sufferings of others, has a therapeutic effect. As John Lawlor points out, "The bedrock of understanding is in shared experience."[67] Lear, therefore, at his death lacks the *tragic* dimension because his concern, unlike that of the heroes in conventional tragedy, is not with his own demise but with another's—Cordelia's. Though his physical condition and especially his mind have deteriorated to the point that he is no longer able to sustain his life, his spiritual development remains intact. The physical and mental relapse that precedes his death, rather than diminishing his human estate, ironically testifies that he has attained a level of being that transcends personal existence. Maynard Mack interestingly comments upon Lear's anti-heroic death and its uniqueness among Shakespeare's tragedies:

> . . .How differently death comes to Lear! Not in a moment of self-scrutiny that stirs us to awe or exaltation or regret at waste, but as a blessing at which we must rejoice with Kent, hardly more than a needful afterthought to the death that counts dramatically, Cordelia's. To die with no salute to death, with the whole consciousness launched toward another; to die following a life-experience in which what we have been shown to admire is far more the capacity to endure than to perform: this is unique in Shakespeare, and sits more easily with our present sensibility (which is pathologically mistrustful of heroism) than the

---

[66]*Ibid.*, p. 130.

[67]John Lawlor, *The Tragic Sense in Shakespeare* (London: Chatto & Windus, 1960), p. 180.

heroic resonances of the usual Shakespearean close.[68]

Whereas Greek tragedy attests that wisdom is attained only by suffering and that man's sorry plight cannot yield any lasting happiness, Shakespearean drama, culminating in *King Lear*, shows "a better way." Through *therapeusis*, it accomplishes not only emotional purgation, but subsequent enlightenment, self-knowledge, and moral edification; but most important, it amplifies our souls, restores psychic harmony, ratifies the bond of humanity, and discloses the spiritual dimension of life. It invites us, in our "wall'd prison" to "take upon's the mystery of things, as if we were God's spies."

---

[68]Mack, *King Lear in Our Time*, p. 84.

BIBLIOGRAPHY

Books

Aristotle, *Poetics.*, tr. S. H. Butcher. New York: Hill and Wang, 1961.

Battenhouse, Roy W. *Shakespearean Tragedy: Its Art and Its Christian Premises.* Bloomington, Ind.: Indiana University Press, 1969.

Bonheim, Helmuth (ed.) *The King Lear Perplex.* San Francisco: Wadsworth Publishing Co., Inc., 1960.

Bradley, A. C. *Shakespearean Tragedy.* Second Edition. London: Macmillan and Co., 1905.

Brooke, Nicholas. "The Ending of *King Lear,*" *Shakespeare 1564-1964.* Ed. Edward Bloom. Providence: Brown University Press, 1964.

Clemen, W. H. *The Development of Shakespeare's Imagery.* Cambridge, Mass.: Haravard University Press, 1951.

Colie, Rosalie L., and F. T. Flahiff. *Some Facets of "King Lear': Essays in Prismatic Criticism.* Toronto: University of Toronto Press, 1974.

Corrigan, Robert W. (ed.) *Comedy: Meaning and Form.* San Francisco: Chandler Publishing Co., 1965.

Coursen, Herbert R., Jr. *Christian Ritual and the World of Shakespeare's Tragedies.* Cranbury, N.J.: Associated University Presses, Inc., 1976.

Cutts, John P. *The Shattered Glass: A Dramatic Pattern in Shakespeare's Early Plays.* Detroit: Wayne State University Press, 1968.

Danson, Lawrence (ed.) *On King Lear.* Princeton: Princeton University Press, 1981.

_____. *Tragic Alphabet: Shakespeare's Drama of Language.* New Haven: Yale University Press, 1974.

Elton, William R. *King Lear and the Gods.* San Marino, Calif.: Huntington Library Publications, 1966.

Frye, Northrop. *Anatomy of Criticism.* Princeton: Princeton University Press, 1957.

_____. *Fools of Time: Studies in Shakespearean Tragedy.* Toronto: University of Toronto Press, 1967.

Frye, Roland. *Shakespeare and Christian Doctrine.* Princeton: Princeton University Press, 1963.

Heilman, Robert Bechtol. *This Great Stage: Image and Structure in King Lear.* Baton Rouge: Louisiana State University Press, 1948.

Hobson, Alan. *Full Circle: Shakespeare and Moral Development.* New York: Barnes & Noble, Inc., 1972.

Horowitz, David. *Shakespeare: An Existential View.* New York: Hill and Wang, 1965.

Knight, G. Wilson. *The Shakespearean Tempest.* London: Methuen & Co., 1953.

_____. *The Wheel of Fire.* London: Methuen & Co., 1930.

Lawlor, John. *The Tragic Sense in Shakespeare.* London: Chatto & Windus, Ltd., 1960.

Mack, Maynard. *King Lear in Our Time.* Berkeley and Los Angeles: University of California Press, 1965.

McElroy, Bernard. *Shakespeare's Mature Tragedies..* Princeton: Princeton University Press, 1973.

Murry, John Middleton. *Shakespeare..* London: Jonathan Cape, 1936.

Nevo, Ruth. *Tragic Form in Shakespeare.* Princeton: Princeton University Press, 1972.

Nietzsche, Friedrich. *The Philosophy of Nietzsche.* Eds. Bennett A. Cerf, Donald S. Klopfer, and Robert K. Hass. New York: Random House, Inc., 1954.

Orwell, George. *Shooting an Elephant and Other Essays.* New York: Harcourt Brace and Co., 1959.

Pasternak, Boris. *I Remember.* tr. David Magarshack. New York: Pantheon Books Inc., 1959.

Rosen, William. *Shakespeare and the Craft of Tragedy.* Cambridge, Mass.: Harvard University Press, 1967.

Sedgewick, G. G. *Of Irony: Especially in the Drama.* Toronto: University of Toronto Press, 1948.

Shakespeare, William. *The Complete Works of Shakespeare.* ed. George L. Kittredge. Boston: Ginn and Co., 1936.

Sharpe, Robert Boies. *Irony in the Drama.* Chapel Hill: The University of North Carolina Press, 1959.

Spencer, Theodore. *Shakespeare and the Nature of Man.* Second Edition. New York: The Macmillan Co., 1949.

Swinburne, Algernon Charles. *Shakespeare.* London: Oxford University Press, 1909.

Urkowitz, Steven. *Shakespeare's Revision of King Lear.* Princeton: Princeton University Press, 1980.

Articles and Periodicals

Brooke, Tucker. "*King Lear* on the Stage." *Sewanee Review,* XXI (1913), 88-98.

Campbell, Oscar James. "The Salvation of Lear." *English Literary History*, XV (1948), 93-109.

Draper, John W. "The Occasion of *King Lear.*" *Studies in Philology.* XXXIV (1937), 176-185.

French, Carolyn S. "Shakespeare's 'Folly' : *King Lear.*" *Shakespeare Quarterly,* X (1959), 523-29.

Greenfield, Thelma Nelson. "The Clothing Motif in *King Lear.*" *Shakespeare Quarterly,* V (1954), 281-86.

Hardison, O. B., Jr. "Logic Versus the Slovenly World in Shakespearean Comedy." *Shakespeare Quarterly,* XXXI:3 (1980), 311-322.

Maclean, Hugh. "Disguise in *King Lear:* Kent and Edgar." *Shakespeare Quarterly,* II (1960), 49-54.

83

McCullen, Joseph T. "Edgar: The Wise Bedlam." *Shakespeare in the Southwest: Some New Directions,* I, edited by T. J. Stafford (El Paso: Texas Western Press, 1969), 43-55.

Ribner, Irving. "Shakespeare and Legendary History: *Lear* and *Cymbeline.*" *Shakespeare Quarterly,* VII (1956), 47-52.

Salter, K. W. "*Lear* and the Morality Tradition." *Notes and Queries,* CXCIX (1954), 109.

Tolstoy, Leo. "On Shakespeare and the Drama." tr. V. Tcherthoff, *Fortnightly Review,* LXXXVI (1906), 963-83.

Williams, George W. "The Poetry of the Storm in *King Lear.*" *Shakespeare Quarterly,* II (1951), 57-71.

Miracle and mystery plays: 16, 30, 32, 70-71
Misjudgment: 12, 13, 55-57, 58, 59, 60, 76
Modern drama: 11
Morality plays: 16, 44, 70-71, 73; *Everyman,* 29, 33; *Lear* as a morality, 29, 32, 33-45
Murry, John Middleton: 1-2, 1n.

Nature: 5, 6, 37, 38, 48, 49, 72
Nietzsche, Friedrich: 11, 54, 54n.

Objectivity: 21, 27, 51, 53, 57, 58, 59, 60, 61, 62-63, 70
Order: 6, 50, 75
Orwell, George: 2, 3, 4, 4n.
Oswald: 13, 35, 39, 40, 41, 42, 43; as representing gluttony, 41-43
Othello: 12, 58

Paganistic elements in *Lear:* 5, 23, 30, 55, 68n.
Pasternak, Boris: 15, 15n.
Peripeteia: 54, 75, 76, 77
Pide Bull edition: 29
Pity and fear: 9-10, 26; pity, 9ff., 14, 58
Poetics, Aristotle's: 7, 7n., 19-20, 72
Primitivism: 13, 33, Cynic-Stoic, 33
Purgation: 23, 26, 34, 67, 73, 77, 78, 79, 80

Redemption: 6, 78; Lear's, 22
Regan: 5, 13, 14, 25, 30, 33, 36, 37, 38, 39-41, 43, 52, 57, 61, 65-66, 68n.; as representing envy, 39-41

Ribner, Irving: 30, 30n.

Salter, K.W.: 29, 29n.
Sedgewick, G.G.: 49-50, 50n.
See feelingly: 56, 78
Seven Deadly Sins: 34, 34-44, 41, 44
Sharpe, Robert Boies: 48-49, 48n.
Society: 8-12, 13, 48, 77
Spencer, Theodore: 30-32, 31n.
Stasis: 47f., 75
Subjectivity: 13, 21, 27, 51, 52, 53, 57-58, 59-64, 70, 74, 76, 77
Superfluous characters: 1, 3, 34, 43, 44, 62
Swinburne, Algernon: 2, 2n.
Symbiosis: 76, 77

Tate, Nahum: 62-63, 62n.
Thematic conclusions: 6, 55; difficulties, 4, 5; discrepancies, 7; illumination, 26
Therapeusis: 28, 74, 78, 80
Therapeutic: 22, 23, 69, 73, 78, 79
Therapy: 22
Tolstoy, Leo: 2, 3, 24, 62, 62n.
Tragedy: 7, 8, 9, 14, 15-17, 19-28, 29, 30, 32, 44, 54, 55, 57, 58, 62-64, 69-80; tragic isolation, 58-59, 78; tragic protagonist, 74-79

Unities, the Three: 23-24
Urkowitz, Steven: 30n.

Violence on stage: 26
Virtues and Vices in *Lear:* 34, 44-45, 55

Watts, Harold H.: 8, 8n.